ALCOHOLISM: THE HIDDEN ADDICTION

ALCOHOLISM: THE HIDDEN ADDICTION

Ebbe Curtis Hoff, M.D.

Foreword by Frank A. Seixas, M.D.

A CROSSROAD BOOK
The Seabury Press • New York

The Seabury Press
815 Second Avenue
New York, N. Y. 10017

Copyright © 1974 by Ebbe Curtis Hoff
Design by Paula Wiener
Printed in the United States of America

LIBRARY OF CONGRESS CATALOGING IN PUBLICATION DATA

Hoff, Ebbe Curtis, 1906-
    Alcoholism: the hidden addiction.

    "A Crossroad book."
    Bibliography: p.
    1. Alcoholism. I. Title. [DNLM: 1. Alcoholism.
WM274 H694a]
RC565.H58   616.8'61   74-13014
ISBN 0-8164-0248-5

To My Patients and Their Families
and To My Colleagues

Contents

Foreword

My first contact with Dr. Ebbe Curtis Hoff was at the Summer School of Alcohol Studies at Rutgers University, New Jersey, where he for many years presided at the Physicians Institute of that school. Dr. Hoff ran the course as a graduate seminar in the socratic method which demanded of each student that he select a topic of interest and prepare it for the judgment of his colleagues. This impetus to scholarship in medical graduate study was a new one for me, and valuable to all of us in learning what was known in the field of alcoholism of particular interest to physicians, the tremendous role which they could and should play in its diagnosis and treatment, and the tremendous need there was for a turnaround of interest in the medical profession as a whole. His management of these seminars brought us all into contact with a wise and gentle man, whose manner in and out of class was an example of the warm and kindly interest in every human being which is so necessary if one is to be successful in the treatment of alcoholism.

Dr. Hoff's students from that course are now in the front rank of the soldiers who are waging the war against alcoholism around the United States. In addition, he headed the alcoholism activities in the Medical College of Virginia, one of the first institutions which made alcoholism a special interest within the confines of a medical college. His interest in patients and in organization created a network of treatment facilities throughout the state of Virginia—a model which could with profit be followed as the states develop their plans for dealing with this urgent public health problem. He has also sparked much research in the subject.

One outstanding quality of Dr. Hoff, which is apparent to all who come into contact with him, is the deep and abiding religious faith which appears to inform his every action. It is perhaps because of this that he so completely embraced the fundamental aspects of the Alcoholics Anonymous program, which has been the mainstay of successful rehabilitation from alcoholism in this country.

In this volume he traces, in simple and understandable manner, the essence of a medical program for the treatment and rehabilitation of persons with alcoholism founded on this matrix, and illustrates his text with reminiscences about patients, ones who succeeded and ones who failed, in their quest for the one outcome that has so far appeared to be most successful in dealing with this disease—total sobriety.

The wealth of his experience must be taken into account in evaluating the material in this book, apparently but deceptively simple. This story can be of considerable assistance to all who come into contact with people suffering from alcoholism—as family member, physician, counselor, or friend.

FRANK A. SEXIAS, M.D.
Medical Director
National Council on Alcoholism

Preface

This book has been named *Alcoholism: The Hidden Addiction* because alcoholism *is* a complex *addiction* and this serious, progressive disorder must be looked upon as a *drug problem*. In fact, it is the most widespread of all forms of drug abuse; and, of all addictions, it is the most destructive of human happiness, safety, health and, indeed, of life itself. Like a malignancy, alcoholism commonly moves progressively to a fatal termination. The word *hidden* in the title stresses the fact that problem drinking is too often misunderstood and taken lightly. It creeps subtly upon its victim if he *denies* his illness and fails to seek rehabilative therapy or delays such treatment until too late. Moreover, there is a tendency to misapprehend the need for comprehensive, ongoing help and most of all to take refuge in the false hope that one can regain control of alcohol and drink normally again. All of these considerations have determined the title of this volume. It will have served its function if it helps its readers to look at alcoholism realistically and seriously, but with hope for those afflicted by it.

Alcohol has long been a part of our social system and we are accustomed to its availability and use in a way that we are not yet accustomed to that of other drugs. In a sense, alcohol has become domesticated by our long familiarity with it as a beverage. We tend not to be frightened about it, and yet we are confused in many ways about alcohol and alcoholism. In these pages, I have tried to present these issues frankly in the hope of dispelling the conspiracy of silence that has long shrouded questions of alcohol use and misuse: How have cultural attitudes toward alcohol changed? What are the physiological and psychological actions of alcohol and why do people drink or abstain? What are the causes of problem drinking and how can *you* as the reader determine whether you are in danger of becoming or have already become an alcoholic? What must you know to identify a problem drinker in your family? What are the ways in which an alcoholic's condition progresses? How can an alcoholic be brought to effective treatment and what *is* recovery for an alcoholic? Lastly, are there ways to prevent problem drinking in your family, and especially in your children?

There are many to whom I am indebted and whose help I wish to acknowledge. First, as recognized in the Dedication, I am profoundly grateful to my patients and their families. My close relations with them over the years have made immensely rewarding a journey into a pioneer and growing field. On this journey, I have come to know at Yale, Rutgers, and here in Virginia a host of students and many elect colleagues to whom I record my thanks. Each of them knows the ties of love and tenderness that bind me to them.

I wish especially to accord warmest thanks to Arthur Buckley, Consultant Editor and Robert Gilday, Editor of *The Seabury Press* for their friendship, advice, and essential help in the preparation of this book. I am grateful to my secretary, Mrs. Gladys Stopes, for skillfully typing the manuscript. I acknowledge thankfully the day-to-day support of my secretary, Mrs. Joyce Parker, who has lightened a labor of authorship that has had to be sandwiched between the tasks of directing a busy clinical program. She has also helped prepare the list of references. Finally, I thank my wife, Phebe, with whom I have shared a life of deep felicity at Oxford, London, New Haven and Richmond. As an elect colleague also, she too, knows my feeling of affectionate obligation.

All of these have made this a better book. For its inadequacies, I must bear full responsibility. My reward will be that you who read it may be inspired to help others, or to find help for yourselves.

E.C.H.

Medical College of Virginia
Virginia Commonwealth University
Richmond, Virginia

PART I
The Drug Alcohol

1
The Unacknowledged Drug

Most people who use alcoholic beverages, especially in a moderate, responsible way, hardly think of their drinking as a form of drug taking. Traditionally, alcohol is viewed merely as a beverage, even though, like drugs, it causes mood changes, such as mental relaxation or exaggerated feelings. The concept of alcohol as a drug, however, is not generally accepted.

Misconceptions about Alcohol

Public interest in drug abuse has expanded enormously of late. This concern is commendable and necessary, but not to the neglect of alcohol problems. We must remember that alcohol too is a drug, and alcohol problems are indeed the most serious and wide-spread of all drug abuse. Though we recognize that there are fads in public attention to medical and social problems, it would be most desirable if we did not have to give primacy to *either* alcohol problems *or* other drug problems, but might approach the two as inevitably interrelated.

There are many people today who seek to find in drugs profound and transcendent experiences. Some believe that

3

these so-called psychedelic explorations result in superior insights and better understanding of the self. Such drug experiences range from marijuana, a relatively mild drug, to LSD, a much more potent one. There are also a number of other drugs that powerfully affect the mind, elevating the mood, subduing undesirable emotions, and calling forth quite profound changes in the way in which the mind deals with reality. The drug alcohol is similarly used in an attempt to expand the mind and to intensify internal experiences.

Early in history men discovered that when they reached the peak of a high mountain they felt as if they had transcended their ordinary selves and were very near the gods. We know today that those feelings were due to the way in which reduction of oxygen tension in the atmosphere depresses the functions of the brain and that, of course, human beings are really no closer to the gods on a mountain than at sea level. Men also discovered very early that alcohol produced somewhat similar feelings. It is hardly surprising, then, that there have been, and still are, religions based upon the use of wine and other drugs. In ancient times there were the various Dionysian cults; today there are still Indians in the Southwest who seek vivid experiences of closeness to God by the controlled ritualistic use of peyote.

Of the drugs we know about that impart transcendent experiences, alcohol is perhaps the most versatile and unpredictable. That is, any given drinking experience depends in part upon the expectations of the one who takes the alcohol. The early phases of the experience may well be associated with a feeling of mental exhilaration, a sense that one is capable, powerful, and even omnipotent. As the experience progresses, however, one becomes more confused and one's thinking deteriorates, often quite abruptly. It has been said that some alcoholics "seek God in the bottom of a bottle." But the truth of the matter is that by the time they get to the bottom, they are in no state to find God or anyone else. Thus, those who use alcohol for "mystical" experiences are generally disappointed.

The pharmacological search for mystical experience is not something new in human history, and it is commonly doomed to failure, for such "mystical" experiences as can be found through anoxia (as in high altitudes), starvation, overbreathing, and drugs are of generally limited value and probably have not contributed greatly to the growth and welfare of our species.

It is true that alcohol can be called a "beverage" when consumed moderately in beer, wine, spirits, or mixed drinks. Indeed, it can even be classified as a food in the sense that it can, in a limited way, supply energy to the body. But when we begin to think of alcohol as a drug, we find ourselves concerned about uses that take on a greater or lesser degree of abnormality. Even in a social setting, in which many feel that alcoholic beverages are not only harmless but also may serve to enhance the interpersonal relationships of an attractive life, the fact remains that a person who downs five highballs or as many cocktails within a couple of hours does become intoxicated and shows unmistakable disturbance of bodily functions and emotional expression. Whether he knows it or not, alcohol is affecting him *as a drug*. And we do know enough today to realize that people, who, for one reason or another, employ alcohol seriously as a psychoactive drug are setting themselves on a dangerous course.

At present, customs associated with the use of alcohol are rapidly changing, and attitudes toward "drinking" are being modified. But it cannot yet be said that the changes are converging in one clear direction. For example, it appears that more people in the United States use alcoholic beverages now than formerly, but that the consumption per capita is somewhat less. It also appears that there is an increasing use of beer over spirits, and that the home as the place to drink is more widely accepted. At the same time, there is a growing need for understanding the extent to which alcohol, when taken as a drug, becomes potentially a serious social, medical, psychological and/or psychiatric problem.

Resulting Confusion and Conspiracy of Silence

The crucial questions that often appear to be too complicated for individuals or society as a whole to answer satisfactorily, are:

1. Exactly when, where, with whom, and how much drinking can be said to be harmless and even socially beneficial? Under what conditions and to what extent does the use of alcoholic liquors point to "danger ahead"?

2. What social attitude, ranging all the way from outright, 100 percent ban at one extreme, to total "permissiveness" or laissez faire at the other, is the wisest and most appropriate course for a society to adopt in dealing with so complex an issue?

Although we hear considerable discussion of the multiple problems related to the use of alcohol, from both medical and social viewpoints, the greatest *single problem*, perhaps, is the lack of agreement as to whether the use of alcohol in general is acceptable or not. This very lack of consensus is in itself a source of great difficulty for many people who, unable or unwilling to think through the many pros and cons for themselves, tend to feel anxiety and guilt over their decision "to drink or not to drink," irrespective of which course they take.

Despite substantial increase in recent years of both scientific knowledge and popular appreciation of the nature of alcohol, there is still much research needed to determine the precise overall and long-term effects of its use. Our society's failure to reach a consensus, however, is due not only to ignorance, but also to a tendency on the part of American people to *avoid coming to grips* with the issue. As a nation, we seem still to be caught between an unwholesome emotionalism about drinking habits on the one hand, and a denial of the need to resolve our differences on the other.

This avoidance is partially understandable because people have been subjected to so many acrimonious and conflicting arguments for and against drinking that they simply go their individual ways, drinking or not as they please, and refuse to discuss their views either privately or publicly. Thus, there has arisen a kind of *conspiracy of silence,* which may relieve people's minds and feelings but which at the same time tends to deprive us of the intelligent base we need if we are to approach alcohol problems effectively. Confronted with highly difficult problems, people tend to give up and become apathetic.

It is the purpose of this book to break this silence—first by examining briefly but as objectively as possible the emotionalism about drinking which, as we shall see, has deep roots in our ethnic, psychological, and religious backgrounds. We shall then go on to a discussion of alcohol—its use, misuse, and nonuse; whether or not there is what we may call a "normal" use of alcoholic beverages and, if so, how it can be distinguished from the kind of use that generates serious problems; what is meant by the term "social drinking" as contrasted with "problem drinking"; and the relation of less serious forms of "problem drinking" to its most serious form which we call "alcoholism." These are all issues that have been prominent throughout American history and yet still remain culturally unresolved.

2
Social Attitudes toward Alcohol

The variety of attitudes toward the use of alcohol, which we have noted, is not only a present-day phenomenon.

Although emphasis might differ from region to region and from one walk of life to another, there has always been a considerable degree of acceptance of drinking even though a vigorous movement in favor of temperance and/or abstinence has also run its course through our history.

National Attitudes Historically

In the colonial period, alcohol, especially "spirits" (produced by distillation of fermented liquors, e.g. whiskey, as distinguished from wines which are produced by fermentation only) was a prominent item of trade. By the time of the American Revolution, drunkenness among soldiers in the Continental Army was recognized as a "problem" and a matter of great concern. In response to that situation, Benjamin Rush (1745–1813), distinguished physician and a signer of the Declaration of Independence, published in 1778 a pamphlet entitled "An Inquiry into the Effects of Spirituous Liquors on the Human Body and Mind." This pamphlet was very influential, and by

1850 something over 200,000 copies of it had been distributed.

As the American nation grew, varied attitudes toward alcohol emerged, stemming largely from the national and religious backgrounds and the social conditions surrounding pioneer life. Expansion into the western parts of the country provided a setting conducive to alcohol use; in keeping with the violet physical aspects of pioneering, excessive drinking led to still greater violence and was often destructive. The ubiquitous saloon and habitual drunkenness in western towns shocked the more established areas of the country.

Simultaneously, active temperance and abstinence societies developed. The Society of Friends took a stand against intemperance early in the colonial period; and as the Methodist movement grew, it also opposed the use of alcoholic beverages. The first permanent temperance society was founded in New York State in 1808; and in 1826 the American Society for the Promotion of Temperance was organized in Boston. The latter society had the support and approval of Presbyterian, Methodist, Congregational, and Baptist bodies, as well as of many individual members of other churches. By 1833 the Society had more than six thousand local branches with over one million members; its enormous strength can be inferred from these figures. As liberals were attracted to the movement, it came to be linked very often with the fight against slavery and various other campaigns for social action.

It is noteworthy that in the early stages of the temperance movement total abstinence was not necessarily obligatory for members. Those who advocated complete abstention from alcoholic beverages worked side by side with those who permitted the moderate use of beer, wine, and other fermented beverages; but all were united against the consumption of distilled spirits. There was also little effort at first to influence public legislation. In fact, many church people felt that the church's task was one of converting and educating the individual, and not one of legislative campaigns; they would leave the social issues of alcohol to the individual conscience. But by 1836 the Society required a binding pledge of all members to work for total abstinence from beverages that could intoxicate. In 1840 the Society even went on record as opposing the use of wine in the Communion service. As a result of the Society's eventual legislative programs, by 1855 thirteen states and territories prohibited by law the sale of liquor. During the War Between the States, however, this control was relaxed and by 1870 only two states had such laws.

The next twenty years witnessed a vigorous revival of the abstinence movement: in 1869 the Prohibition Party was founded; in 1874 the Women's Christian Temperance Union; and in 1895 the Anti-Saloon League was organized at Oberlin, Ohio. As a result of their renewed activities, by 1916 statewide prohibition laws existed in nineteen states, with local option laws in twenty-six other states. Nationwide prohibition came into effect through the ratification of the Eighteenth Amendment on January 16, 1920, but was repealed in 1933. At the present time, most states have alcohol education councils working in cooperation with the American Council on Alcohol Problems, with headquarters in Washington, D.C. Many of these bodies have altered their names to express their new concept of function, i.e., education about alcohol and other drug problems.

Unfortunately, what we have called the "conspiracy of silence" which prevents free and candid discussion of our conflicting views has also had the effect for many years of turning public attention away from support of scientific research on alcohol use and alcohol problems. Yet in the past few years this trend has been considerably reversed; and it is greatly to be hoped that questions of drinking, nondrinking, and alcohol abuse will in the future receive their rightful attention consistent with the seriousness of the problem.

Cultural Sanction of Use

As alcohol is a drug problem, "drug abuse" and "alcoholism" should be compared, although preventive and therapeutic techniques may be different.

One of the special issues relating to alcohol use as distinct from other kinds of drug use, however, is that alcohol use is *culturally sanctioned*, whereas certain drug uses are regarded as abnormal and indeed are punishable as illegal. Sale of alcohol is legally controlled, and alcohol may be consumed without breaking the law; whereas marijuana and LSD are illegal, and those who use them are subject to prosecution.

This difference between alcohol and other drugs is one of concern to many young people, some of whom have come to the conclusion that alcohol use can be a rather unproductive and even besotted kind of behavior, whereas the practice of using marijuana, LSD, and other psychedelic drugs can expand the mind and enhance research, particularly private investigation into the depths of personality. In the 60s, such attitudes were popular, yet just now there appears to be a reduction in the use of LSD and heroin in favor of marijuana and alcohol. In our clinic, over the past five years we have witnessed a selective increase in addictive use of alcohol by young people.

When an individual cannot resolve his drinking problem, continuation of the practice almost always involves a sense of guilt. It has been estimated that about a third of the adults in the United States believe that the use of alcoholic beverages is wrong, and that such beverages should not be made or sold to the public. On the other hand, some seventy million or more people in the United States do use alcoholic beverages in one form or another, either occasionally or regularly. Many are doing so without a very clear idea of why they do or what constitutes appropriate use. Attitudes range from moderate sanction to heavy continual use. Ironically, some habitual drinkers are among those who feel the most guilt about their practice.

Young people as well as adults differ in their attitudes about drinking. Some young people come from homes where a moderate use of alcohol is normative and where a glass of beer or wine is a regular custom, whereas for others the normal practice at home is abstinence. For still other people, home life has been complicated by heavy drinking or alcoholism in the family. It is not surprising then, that both young people and adults resent comments on their attitudes about alcohol, partly because they are so sensitive about the matter and partly because they see such comments as attempts to interfere with their own freedom of behavior.

I believe that one of the difficulties encountered in any attempt to change attitudes about drinking and drug use is that in America the stress upon "selling" ideas as well as products is so unremitting that we tend to become immune to all "persuaders." We are particularly resentful when it appears that the "persuaders" are trying to limit our enjoyment of life in order to perpetuate old-fashioned, outworn beliefs. We live in times of polarization when people seem to be strongly "for" or "against." If we are to comprehend the problems connected with alcohol, it is imperative that we understand the justifications offered for *all* shades of opinion, from the "pros" demanding total acceptance to the "cons" who will be satisfied with nothing less than total abstinence.

Opposition to Alcohol

Those who really oppose drinking do so for a variety of reasons. Among the main ones are these: *(a)* drinking is sinful or

immoral; *(b)* drinking is bad for the health; *(c)* drinking up-
sets family life, work efficiency, and community welfare; *(d)*
drinking leads to alcoholism; and *(e)* drinking causes traffic
and industrial accidents (McCarthy [1]). For these reasons,
many people believe that for the good of society and of individuals the production and sale of alcoholic beverages
should be forbidden by law or carefully restricted, and that
people be warned and encouraged *not* to drink.

This is a formidable list of attitudes which must be calmly
considered. As to the morality of alcohol use, there has been
for centuries a prevailing tradition in the Christian church and
certainly in Judaism that there is a proper use of alcoholic
beverages; that is to say, a responsible use in which one gives
grateful and joyful thanks to God. Within this tradition, however, drinking is wrong when it is irresponsible, when it is
gluttonous indulgence, when it separates man from his closeness to God (as happens when people become drunk), when
it harms man as the temple of the Holy Spirit and when it
harms his relationships with his fellow human beings.

Opposition to drinking is often paramount in the minds of
those who feel that the introduction of distilled spirits into the
drinking culture has been a factor in perpetuating alcohol
problems. Traditional Old Testament biblical acceptance of responsible drinking must be assessed, however, in light of
early ignorance of the process and now widespread use of
distillation. The demands of industrialized society also have
changed people's attitudes toward drinking. Today the consumption of spirits can subject people to greater hazards such
as traffic accidents on a grand scale. There is no question about
the terrible dangers of operating a car or any other complicated power machinery under the influence of alcohol.

Drunkenness is associated with serious disturbances of
health and family life and with crime, poverty, and violence.
Most scientists take the view, however, that scientific evidence

has not yet established a connection between these evils and moderate use of alcoholic beverages. Moreover, as we shall see, the causes of alcoholism and other problem drinking are very complex and not completely understood.

It is an oversimplification to say that drinking causes alcoholism. Community acceptance of *drunken behavior* seems to be positively related to the prevalence of alcoholism. Although we have made some progress in identifying vulnerable members of a population (that is to say, those who are more than likely to succumb to drinking problems), we do not yet know how to predict with complete accuracy who will or will not become a problem drinker. As we shall see there are physiological, biochemical, and psychological factors as as well as social and cultural ones, which help us in our predictions.

Advocacy of Controlled Use

A parallel list of attitudes of those who believe that alcohol may serve a good purpose may be constructed: *(a)* moderate and responsible use of alcohol in small amounts does not harm the individual or society; *(b)* it is drunkenness which is sinful or immoral, drinking in itself is not; *(c)* the disturbances resulting from drunkenness are committed by a small number of offenders; *(d)* alcoholism is not caused by alcohol only; and *(e)* the decision to drink or not to drink should be made by the individual and not determined by law.

Of course, as we have pointed out, there are many who accept drinking whose views, if they have any at all about the matter, are extremely naïve and poorly thought through. In our home we have a practice of saying the grace in the evening before the cocktail hour on the principle that the meal begins at that time. Some of our guests find this an attractive custom while others—although they are happy to have a drink—are not quite sure whether it is appropriate to bless God in this fashion. My personal feeling about the latter guests (and sometimes when I know them well enough, I venture to express it) is that if they are not willing to say grace over their cocktail, they had better reexamine their position and either not drink at all or else explore in all seriousness their acceptance of responsibility for themselves and others and their relation to God himself.

In the above list of justifications offered by the "pros," we encounter the expressions "moderate use" and "small amounts." People who decide not to drink at all do not face the problem of the definition of "moderate use" but those who do sincerely believe that there is a right and proper use have to examine this question carefully. They have to find out what they mean by moderation and, as we have stated before, this question has been discussed by many, including Fr. John C. Ford (2) who stresses the point that moderate use properly includes the objectives of relaxation and social relationships but not getting a "jolt" or a "blast" or any other violent effect.

It is true that there are biblical sources that can be validly interpreted as indicating that drinking in a moderate responsible fashion is acceptable. Drunkenness is always referred to in Scripture as sinful, immoral, and an offense against God ("Nor . . . drunkards, . . . shall inherit the kingdom of God. And such were some of you: . . ."—I Cor. 6:10-11). Regarding this matter of the disturbances resulting from drunkenness, we really ought to ask ourselves how tolerant we, as individuals and as groups in society, can be or ought to be of the disturbances that do result from drunkenness—even, as this list would have us believe, if caused by "a small number of offenders." I do not suppose that there are any reliable figures as to the number of people who get drunk each day or each year in the United States or in other countries of the world. We know something about the number of drunkenness offenders who are apprehended by police, and these figures are large.

The question of our tolerance of drunkenness is important and the question is answered differently by different cultural and national groups. Actually drunkenness, whether of sick alcoholics or those who are not alcoholics, is very costly to society in a variety of ways: road and industrial accidents; absenteeism from work; court, police, and prison costs; and above all human disorganization and misery. The fact remains that people who get drunk become irresponsible, unpredictable people who may be a hazard to themselves and to others and, who are at best a source of anxiety to their families and friends. The work of Dr. E. M. Jellinek (3) on French and Italian groups would seem to show that there was a cause-and-effect relationship between sanction against drunkenness in the latter national group and the relatively low rate of alcoholism in Italy at the time of Jellinek's study. These studies are indeed provocative and suggest that public disapproval of drunken behavior may well be an essential deterrent in preventing or reducing incidence of alcoholism and other forms of problem drinking.

Undoubtedly, the intoxicating and exhilarating effects of fermented mixtures have been known to man since the dawn of history. Primitive people consumed all kinds of juices and rotting fruit as well as the leaves, bark, roots, flowers, and seeds of plants, and in the course of this experimentation they encountered not only ethyl alcohol but also substances like opium with definite medicinal properties and psychological effects. Fermented drinks were found to give feelings of joy and finally, if enough were taken, to put the drinker to sleep. It was not unusual among primitive people to seek and experience the full spectrum of alcohol effects when they drank. This is still normative behavior in some cultures.

Even before historical times and doubtless even before the emergence of man in the evolutionary process, ethyl alcohol was taken into the diet. This is evidenced by the fact that there are enzymes in the body which specifically catalyze (that is to say, accelerate and assist in) the breakdown of alcohol. The earliest records of ancient civilization contain commentaries on alcoholic drinks and discuss their use— both proper and improper—as well as special restrictions upon their use by certain persons and at certain times and places. Alcoholic beverages have always been recognized as potent substances over which society should exercise a measure of control. As far as we know, virtually all societies and cultures have had problems with the pathological use of alcohol. Drunkenness and alcoholism, as we understand these terms today, have presented difficulties from the beginning. I know of no cultures in which alcohol has *never* been used, though there may have been a possible exception in the pre-Columbian Indian tribes of North America, who lived in the area now constituting most of the continental United States, of whom it has been said that alcohol was either never used or used only sporadically and in isolated places.

The preparation and drinking of fermented liquors has been one of the commonest practices of man in virtually all civilizations. Drinking has had religious connotations and it has been considered a source of health and strength. The latter idea still persists strongly in many parts of the world. Certainly the use of alcoholic beverages is now established universally in spite of the fact that there are some legal, cultural, and religious restrictions of it. In fact, we all know that drinking is practiced even by members of religious bodies which formally forbid it. Thus some Moslems rationalize the use of alcoholic beverages, and it is also quite common among large numbers affiliated with Christian denominations, the formal disciplinary statements of which require members to abstain. The views of Christian denominations toward drinking have been liberalized considerably within the past few years, at least by some of their leaders.

Facing the Issue

There is no question, as has been pointed out, that many people in our country do use alcoholic beverages in spite of their feeling that they are doing wrong. Somehow they manage to reassure themselves that they are not doing "too wrong." My feeling is not only that such questions of ethics and behavior are to be answered within the framework of personal and interpersonal responsibility, but also that the ethical position one takes about alcohol, drug use, and other comparable issues must be guided by the best scientific knowledge available. For example, if it can be conclusively shown that smoking cigarettes is a serious health hazard, then the ethical position with respect to smoking becomes quite obvious since it is ethically wrong knowingly to damage one's own body and mind.

In summary, the issues we face in deciding whether "to drink or not to drink" are much more profound than many people—even today—seem to realize. Those who oversimplify the issues frequently find themselves in embarrassing and indeed heretical positions. Others are anxiously trying to make intelligent decisions and to formulate for themselves a viable attitude toward alcohol use that will not only determine their own practices but help them to guide those of their children. But they often find, quite justifiably, that under the bombardment of educational material on alcohol and drugs, to which most of us have been subjected, it is hard to judge what is mere emotional propaganda and what can be trusted as scientifically valid. They ask, What is really known about alcohol use and abuse, and what is still conjecture?

My answer is that accurate scientific knowledge is indeed indispensable, and that we do have available, here and now, many valid and helpful answers to their questions. We are far from knowing all that we would like about some of the more complex problems, but we are able, as a result of scientific research over the past few years, to sort out many entirely trustworthy facts.

The simplest of these, and at the same time the most fundamental, are the basic chemical and physiological realities which are the subject of our next chapter. Building on this foundation, we shall then discuss more complicated aspects of alcohol use which have their roots in family life, in the development of human personality, and in community aspirations and goals as they are expressed through and affected by life's day-to-day experiences. I make a solemn plea for patience and resourcefulness, for honest and open discussion among those holding diverse views, and for continuing research and study at every level and on an interdisciplinary basis.

3
The Properties
of Alcohol

Throughout this book when we use the word alcohol we refer to *ethyl alcohol*. This is the essential substance present in wine, beer, and distilled spirits, which gives them their most characteristic properties.

The Substance

Ethyl alcohol (known chemically as *ethanol*) is expressed by the formula C_2H_5OH. A molecule of ethyl alcohol is composed of two atoms of carbon, six atoms of hydrogen, and one of oxygen. Other alcohols exist—for example, methyl alcohol (wood alcohol, CH_3OH) and so-called *higher* alcohols with three, four, five, or more carbon atoms in the molecule. Methyl alcohol is well known as a dangerous poison. These higher alcohols are present in small amounts in alcoholic beverages usually referred to as *congeners*. Some studies of congeners indicate that they may have some inebriating effect upon the human being, but essentially the effects of alcoholic beverages can be ascribed to the ethyl alcohol which they contain. Therefore, it is about ethyl alcohol that we shall be speaking in this chapter on what alcohol is and does.

Pure alcohol is a light, colorless fluid with a slight but aromatic odor and a burning, pungent taste. Chemically it is not unlike ether, $C_2H_5OC_2H_5$, which as the formula shows, is also made up only of carbon, hydrogen, and oxygen—the elements present in water (H_2O), air (oxygen, O_2), and carbon dioxide (CO_2). Thus alcohol is a simple molecule formed from some of the most common elements around us. Like ether also, alcohol is probably best described as an anesthetic. Although alcohol acts upon a variety of cells and tissues of the body, most of its effects upon intellect, feelings, and behavior can be explained by its anesthetic action upon cells of the central nervous system called *neurons*. We shall see that this action appears to work progressively, affecting certain nerve cells earlier and others later, as the concentration of the alcohol in the blood supplying the brain rises. Thus the action of alcohol upon neurons is characteristically an anesthetic, depressing or numbing one. However, since nerve cells are linked together in both inhibitory and excitatory circuits, situations can and do develop in which alcohol depresses an *inhibitory* circuit; therefore, for a time it will have the converse effect on the brain, and hence on behavior, and will produce excitement. For this reason alcohol is often thought of as a *stimulant*. Such stimulant action is a temporary effect of alcohol on the brain system and does not gainsay the fact that alcohol is a depressant or anesthetic in its action upon a given nerve cell.

Alcohol is produced in nature by a process known as *fermentation*. This is a biochemical action by which small microscopic yeast cells (present in the air and lying on the surface of fruits and grains) change sugar into alcohol and carbon dioxide. Fermented, alcohol-containing fruits and cereals have formed a part of the diet of man and animals over the ages, as evidenced by enzymes in the liver and other organs which specifically take part in the breakdown of alcohol ingested by the body. The chemical reaction by which grape sugar is turned to alcohol is as follows: $C_6H_{12}O_6$ leads to $2C_2H_5OH$ plus $2CO_2$, i.e., grape sugar forms alcohol plus carbon dioxide. In any actively fermenting mixture, the carbon dioxide can be observed in the form of bubbles. In sparkling wines, like champagne, CO_2 goes into solution under pressure, giving the wine its sharp, bubbly character and acid taste. Given enough sugar in the fermenting mixture, the fermentation process will continue until the alcohol content rises to approximately 14 percent (by volume). At this stage, the yeast cells stop working so that there is a natural limit to the concentration that can be reached in fermentation. Moreover, if an alcohol mixture such as wine is left in the open, a further process is initiated by which certain bacteria change the alcohol into acetic acid (vinegar). Thus wine will turn sour unless preventive steps are taken. The eminent French scientist Pasteur discovered that killing the bacteria by heating wine to a certain temperature before corking it would prevent souring. This process known as "pasteurization" also destroys disease microorganisms and is commonly used in rendering milk safe to drink.

There are many kinds of alcoholic beverages. *Wine* is made from grapes or other fruits and berries and may have an alcohol content as high as 12 to 14 percent. Some wines, such as sherry, are "fortified" (given a higher alcoholic content) by adding brandy or grain alcohol. *Beers* and *ales* are prepared by fermenting a broth made from malted grains. The starch in the grain is converted to sugar and the yeast acts upon the sugar. Hops are usually added to give the beverage a characteristic bitter taste. Beers contain some 3 to 6 percent alcohol, the average in the United States being about 4.5 percent.

Distilled spirits are made by heating wine or other fermented mixtures in an apparatus called a *still*. Since alcohol has a lower boiling point than water, the alcohol boils off first.

This is condensed in the cooling coils of the still and is collected. In this way a concentrated alcohol solution up to 95 percent can be prepared. Various kinds of *whiskey* (from the Gaelic word *usquebaugh,* meaning "water of life") are distilled from fermented mixtures of cereals or potatoes and usually contain 40 to 50 percent alcohol. A 50-percent mixture is spoken of as "100 proof," a term derived from an old way of testing or "proving" the strength of the whiskey: a mixture of this strength when poured on gunpowder will not prevent the powder from burning when ignited. Today the "proof" is given as twice the alcohol percentage: a 45-percent whiskey is spoken of as 90 proof, a 40-percent as 80 proof, and so on. *Gin* is distilled *neutral spirits* (a 40- to 50-percent solution) flavored with juniper berries. *Vodka* is distilled from rye, barley, or potatoes and has no flavor; it is usually a 40- to 50-percent solution. *Rum* is made from molasses or cane sugar and has an alcohol content that may reach 70- to 90-percent. *Brandy* is distilled from wine and can be sweetened and flavored to make *liqueurs* or *cordials.*

Its Physiological Effects

Alcohol can enter the body in various ways. It can be introduced into the bloodstream by intravenous injection, a method used for medical or scientific purposes. It can also be injected into the area around certain nerves or given by enema. Small amounts can enter the body by inhalation and absorption through the lungs, and minute amounts get into the system when large areas of the skin are rubbed with alcohol. Alcoholic beverages, of course, are taken by mouth, in either diluted or concentrated forms. When taken without dilution, distilled beverages cause a burning sensation in the mouth and gullet, and most alcoholic drinks, as commonly used, give a sensation of warmth as they are swallowed. The somewhat irritating effects of concentrated alcoholic drinks in the mouth and throat may cause an immediate though slight rise in blood pressure or heart rate. But salivation stimulated by alcoholic drinks, causes the concentrated drinks to be diluted quickly.

It appears that little or no alcohol is absorbed into the bloodstream through the membranes of the mouth and that absorption does not really begin until the beverage reaches the stomach. In fact, the absorption of alcohol through the stomach wall is slow and incomplete and only about 30 to 40 percent of the alcohol reaching the stomach is indeed absorbed there. Alcohol in concentrations greater than 4 to 5 percent is diluted by the gastric juice on reaching the stomach.

We have said that alcohol is a food in the sense that, in a limited way, it can supply energy to the body. However, it is different from most foods in that it does not require digestion and is absorbed unchanged into the blood through the walls of the alimentary tract. (Also, to qualify as a "food," a substance must have other properties besides merely producing immediate energy.) Sixty to 70 percent of the alcohol which one drinks enters the bloodstream by the intestines. Here the process of absorption is swifter and more thorough and less variable than in the stomach. If alcohol is taken on an empty stomach, the substance tends to pass rapidly into the intestines and from there is quickly taken up by the blood. This is why a drink taken before or without a meal tends to have a proportionately greater "kick" in relation to the amount taken. Certain foods in the stomach, especially fats and proteins, tend to slow down the stomach's emptying time so that absorption from the intestines is delayed; thus alcoholic beverages taken after a meal have less effect in proportion to the amount drunk. Between the stomach and the intestines is the *pyloric valve,* which may close down, especially if large amounts of alcohol are drunk, so that there may be not only delay of the passage of alcohol into the intestines, but also vomiting so that the contents of the stomach are ejected from the body. Sometimes alcohol may be retained in the stomach for several hours and then on reaching the intestines cause *delayed intoxication*.

If a person has been fasting, alcohol usually enters the blood quite quickly, that is to say, within a few minutes. The alcohol is carried first, by way of the veins, from the stomach and the intestines to the liver, and from there to the heart, then to the lungs and back to the heart again; and finally, it is pumped by the heart through the arteries to all the tissues of the body, including the brain, becoming evenly distributed in all body cells and fluids.

Let us now follow the ways in which the body handles this alcohol that has been absorbed into the bloodstream and distributed through tissues and fluids: (1) about 2 percent—or in heavy indulgence as much as 10 percent— of the absorbed alcohol is excreted, relatively unchanged, from the lungs. (The odor on the breath of a person who has been drinking is evidence of such excretion.) There is also some excretion in the urine and feces and, in relatively small amounts, in sweat and tears; (2) the rest of the alcohol, namely some 90 to 98 percent, is burned (oxidized) to form carbon dioxide and water with release of energy.

This process of breaking down alcohol occurs in stages, beginning in the liver. The essential function of the liver in alcohol metabolism is to break down the alcohol to *acetaldehyde* (by a special enzyme, *alcohol dehydrogenase*). The rest of the process, from acetaldehyde to carbon dioxide and water can take place in any living tissue of the body. But because the breakdown process of alcohol in the liver proceeds at a rate set by that organ, the rate of combustion in the body as a whole is limited thereby; and the liver may be said to act as the "bottleneck" in the process. Thus, if more alcohol enters the bloodstream than the liver can handle, it dams up in the blood and the blood alcohol concentration rises.

Alcohol, we have noted, is like carbohydrates, fats, and proteins in that it can be oxidized to carbon dioxide and water and thus provide heat and energy. There is a difference, however. In the case of ordinary foods, the rate of oxidation is adjusted to the needs of the body, but with alcohol (because of the liver "bottleneck") this adjustment does not occur. Thus, if a person were very hungry and needed energy and tried to obtain it from alcohol, the rate of energy supply might not be adequate for his needs, especially if he were engaging in heavy exercise. It should be noted, too, that the warmth often felt when one drinks is not due to a sudden release of energy to the body but to a dilatation (widening) of the blood vessels of the skin so that warmer blood from the deeper parts of the body comes to the surface. This causes a comforting illusion of warmth. What actually happens, however, is that heat is being lost from the body at a more rapid rate than normal. For this reason, alcohol should not be taken before exposure to extreme cold because this dilatation of skin vessels causes increased heat loss which may be dangerous.

The rate at which alcohol is burned in the body depends primarily upon the total mass of functioning liver tissue. Since the size of the liver in relation to body size is about the same in all people, the proportion of alcohol burned each hour, practically speaking, is the same for all. There is no clearly effective way of changing the rate of breakdown of alcohol; it is the same at rest or in exercise, asleep or awake. Thus, popular ideas of throwing off alcohol more rapidly by various means, such as cold showers or black coffee, are essentially erroneous.

Ordinarily, the human body can burn up about 1 gram of pure alcohol per hour per 10 kilograms of body weight. This corresponds to 1/24 of a fluid ounce per hour for 22 pounds of body weight. It is possible to calculate the rate at which a person will burn alcoholic beverages from the following simple formula: $W/5xP = V$, where W equals the body weight in pounds; P equals the percentage of alcohol by volume in a beverage; and V equals the amount of the beverage in ounces that the person can burn in one hour. From this formula we calculate that a 150-pound person will burn about 3/4 of an ounce of 80-proof whiskey (40 percent by volume) per hour; 2 3/4 ounces of ordinary wine; or 8 1/2 ounces of beer. As has been stated, if alcohol is absorbed more rapidly than it can be excreted by the lungs, kidneys, and so forth, and burned, it increases in concentration in the blood and in the tissue fluids themselves. This concentration continues to increase until most of the alcohol is absorbed. Subsequently, the blood alcohol content falls steadily at the rate of about 0.015 percent per hour until none is left. The chart shown in Figure 1 indicates some of the effects of alcoholic beverages upon an average person weighing 150 pounds. We observe, for example, that a blood alcohol concentration of 0.15 percent means that the equivalent of 1/2 pint of whiskey is present in the body. With such a blood alcohol level, a person is legally "under the influence" in many states; indeed, most people show unmistakable signs of drunkenness at this point. The chart also shows that it takes about 10 hours, in an average person, for all alcohol to leave the body after such a level has been reached. For those weighing considerably more or less, the amount of alcoholic beverage would be proportionately greater or smaller to give the same effects. The effects of the drink diminish as the concentration of alcohol in the blood falls.

The burning of alcohol in the body generates about 7 calories per gram of alcohol. As we have indicated, alcohol's limitation as a food lies in part in the fact that it makes energy available at a restricted rate. Even worse, it causes intoxication when it is consumed in excess of its combustion in the body. It is also unfortunately true that alcohol can be taken in such large amounts as to replace genuine, tissue-building foods; so a person who drinks, for example, a pint of whiskey every day will derive 1,200 calories from it, which may be approximately one-half of his daily requirement. By such a dietary regime (drinking his meals, as it were), a person is seriously depriving himself of necessary vitamins, minerals, and essential proteins. The result of persisting in such a diet is that he will probably become a victim of serious nutritional diseases which may harm the nerves, the brain, the liver, heart, and other organs.

How It Causes Intoxication

The chart shown in Figure 1 has given us a general idea of some of the effects of alcoholic beverages. We now come to the question of how alcohol acts to cause intoxication and certain other effects short of intoxication, and where its main sites of action are. We may generally define acute alcohol intoxication as a disturbance of mental and bodily functions resulting from the presence of alcohol in the central nervous system. It is certainly true that alcohol affects all tissues and organs of the body to some extent, and more particularly if it is consumed regularly over a long period of time. However, it is the acute action upon the brain and hence upon mental and emotional functions, as well as sensory and motor capabilities, that is of particular interest and importance here in our examination of the immediate effects of alcohol.

The range of blood alcohol concentrations in the body causing the wide spectrum of effects, from mild relaxation to coma, is really very small. A person usually loses consciousness when the blood alcohol reaches 0.40 percent—that is to

Figure 1

SOME EFFECTS OF ALCOHOLIC BEVERAGES*

Amount of beverage	Concentration of alcohol attained in the blood	Effects	Time required for all alcohol to leave the body
1 highball (1½ oz. whisky) or 1 cocktail (1½ oz. whisky) or 3½ oz. fortified wine or 5½ oz. ordinary wine or 2 bottles (24 oz.) beer	0.03%	Slight changes in feeling	2 hrs.
2 highballs or 2 cocktails or 7 oz. fortified wine or 11 oz. ordinary wine or 4 bottles beer	0.06%	Increasing effects with variation	Feeling of warmth—mental relaxation—slight decrease of fine skills—less concern with minor irritations and restraints. → 4 hrs.
3 highballs or 3 cocktails or 10½ oz. fortified wine or 16½ oz. (1 pt.) ordinary wine or 6 bottles beer	0.09%	among individuals and in the same	Buoyancy—exaggerated emotion and behavior—talkative, noisy or morose. → 6 hrs.
4 highballs or 4 cocktails or 14 oz. fortified wine or 22 oz. ordinary wine or 8 bottles (3 qts.) beer	0.12%	individual at different times.	Impairment of fine co-ordination—clumsiness—slight to moderate unsteadiness in standing or walking. → 10 hrs. 8 hrs.

| 5 highballs or
5 cocktails or
17½ oz. fortified wine or
27½ oz. ordinary wine or
½ pt. whisky | 0.15% | Intoxication—unmistakable abnormality of gross bodily functions and mental faculties. |

would have to be correspondingly more or less to produce the same results. The effects indicated at each stage will diminish as the concentration of alcohol in the blood is reduced by being oxidized and eliminated.

(From *Decisions About Alcohol*, Seabury Press)

Reproduced by permission from Popular Pamphlet No. 4, "What the Body Does with Alcohol", by Leon A. Greenberg. Copyright 1955 by Journal of Studies on Alcohol, Inc., New Haven, Conn.

* Based on a person of "average" size (150 pounds). For those weighing considerably more or less, the amounts

say, only 40 parts of alcohol in 10,000 parts of blood. If a person drinks, for example, a quart of whiskey rather quickly before passing out, the blood level of alcohol will continue to rise to a percentage around 0.50 and the victim will be perilously near death. At some point between 0.50 and 1.0 percent, the breathing center in the brain stem (medulla) becomes anesthetized, respiration fails, and the person dies.

As our chart shows, a blood level of 0.03 percent, which may be achieved by drinking two bottles of beer or a highball containing 1 1/2 ounces of whiskey, produces some changes in feeling. Such changes are variously described by different alcohol users as euphoria, well-being, or depression; in all cases, if the whiskey or beer is consumed rather slowly—over a period of an hour, for example—the changes will be considerably less. Moreover, having two bottles of beer with a meal will cause less change than if the same amount of beverage is consumed without food. For most people who have been tested, blood levels below 0.02 to 0.03 percent are not generally associated with signs of impaired function. But as we have said, people vary, and since this is the case, there is a definite minority that will be unfavorably affected by these low blood levels and will find their judgment, attention, and emotional balance disturbed. The amount of alcohol taken to cause levels of 0.03 percent or less is burned and cleared from the body within two hours so that the acute disturbance does not last long. It has been suggested that to be on the safe side a member of this minority should not take more than one bottle of beer or one highball an hour during an evening. In order for this strategy to be effective, the alcohol level must be kept below 0.03 percent right from the start. While this is a general precaution, it is, of course, much safer, if one is to drive at the end of an evening, not to drink any alcoholic beverages at all. In countries such as Sweden with strict enforcement of laws regarding alcohol blood levels, guests often decide in advance that the one who will drive home will not do any drinking at the party.

The earliest effects of alcoholic beverages producing blood levels up to 0.03 percent are usually feelings of relaxation and mild sedation. Because one feels less tense, there is often a sense of relief from fatigue and one may be a little less shy in groups, more friendly, more willing to speak and less worried about the problems of the day. Thus the first effects of alcohol in small amounts are mainly psychological and there is no change, or only a minimal change, in one's motor performance. It is as if the alcohol first modified the activity of brain circuits connected with the so-called higher functions, such as judgment, attention, and capacity to be anxious for the future. This action seems to be due, in part at least, to direct effects of lower circuits in the brain influencing the cerebral cortex and other higher centers. As the blood alcohol rises, other parts of the brain are quieted and this progressive numbing effect on brain function goes on until at last the nervous control of breathing is paralyzed.

Anyone who has had any personal experience with drinking or watched the effects of alcohol on others knows that with relatively low alcohol blood levels people generally appear to feel that they are more alert and more capable. This is because anesthesia of brain mechanisms regulating intellectual and emotional control causes them to be less frightened, inhibited, and anxious. For this reason some creative workers sometimes rely upon alcohol for inspiration, courage, and motivation for their work. I have had newspapermen as patients who told me that a drink or two would give them enough motivation to start on a newspaper article on which there was a deadline when they could not otherwise get it underway. Some people find in alcohol a way to dissolve fears about many things, such as examinations, an important interview, or a sexual relation. I remember the story of a patient of mine who told me that when she went to her first dance in college she felt dreadfully shy, out of place, and miserable. Someone brought her a cocktail—the first in her life—and after two of these she felt wonderfully relaxed, happy, and secure, more than she had ever been in her whole life. One can easily see that the use of such a *chemical comforter* or *chemical crutch* can readily become harmful, and this proved to be the case with the patient in question. Having discovered that alcohol could smooth out her worries, troubles, fears, and miseries, she began from the age of nineteen to use alcohol in this way, to the exclusion of important maturing experiences, until she died at the age of about forty, a very heavily addicted alcoholic.

Alcohol is not, of course, the only chemical that can be used in this way. Indeed, an important matter for investigation is to what extent people should or should not rely upon one or another of the several new drugs that control and modify feelings or even alter one's perception of reality. The inappropriate use of psychedelic drugs is one of the most important issues of our time. Not only are there real dangers of addiction when some of these substances are used; but even apart from that problem, there are questions of body and brain damage. Sometimes young people ask if such drugs may not be justified by the possibility that they may offer deeper insight into human personality and so expand human creativeness. While final answers to such questions must depend upon further competent medical and psychological research it can be asserted at this time that the practice of seeking deeper human insights through the use of such drugs is fraught with peril.

Quite striking intellectual and emotional changes will have occurred in an acute drinking episode before noticeable alterations in actual motor skill come about. For example, a person may feel on top of the world and can become a dangerous driver before there is any adverse effect on the actual motor reaction time. Many judges, lawyers, and physicians say that at some point between 0.05 and 0.06 percent alcohol blood level, a person is "under the influence" of alcohol. This state can be reached by drinking two whiskey highballs or four bottles of beer. At such a level not only is judgment impaired but there is also partial numbing of the motor systems of the brain and interference with skilled movements. At levels between 0.09 and 0.12 percent (3 or 4 highballs) the impairment of the motor functions becomes more profound and there is unsteadiness in standing or walking. Sensation is also affected and a person pays less attention to pain, touch, light, and sounds. In Virginia, a person is legally under the influence at 0.10 percent. At a level of 0.15 percent or more of alcohol in the blood there is definite evidence of being under the influence of alcohol and gross incoordination of body movements and mental disturbance increases.

Other Effects on the Human System

We have said that alcohol use for nonalcoholics may amount to nothing much more than a mild relaxant and tension reliever. With many people, alcohol is used in amounts only to reduce anxiety; but if alcohol use develops into uncontrolled alcoholism, anxiety is not really relieved but enhanced. A difficulty which alcoholics experience is that their expectations as to the effects of alcohol are not fulfilled, nor are their expectations and experiences while drinking heavily appropriately apprehended after they become sober—say, during the next few days or a week. Their understanding of their heavy drinking experience is effectively dissociated, as it were, from their sober periods, and this is one of the factors which often makes the therapy of an alcoholic so difficult. The alcoholic does not seem to comprehend fully what happened to him while drunk or drinking heavily and he cannot, therefore, appreciate the nature of his problem. It might be put this way: the drinking experience for an alcoholic *is not a positive learning experience;* and far from leading him into new insights which he can use effectively, it actually deprives him of valuable experiences that he might conceivably have had. The same can be said for the drinking experience of many nonalcoholics. Some people, whether alcoholics or not, simply become active, elated, or even boisterous; others go through these stages first and then become morose and maudlin, tearful and stupid. It has been been said that people tend to reveal their true personality under the influence of alcohol and an old proverb has it: "In wine there is truth." It is probably more accurate, however, to say that the behavior of a person "under the influence" of alcohol is an entirely *new kind of behavior* arising, as it does, from disturbed brain function. For this reason, the person under the influence of alcohol should be said to be, to a greater or less degree, behaving *differently* rather than to be revealing his true self "unmasked." A person under the influence of alcohol is a truncated or limited person.

It is of interest that the overt and subjective effects of drinking may vary according to the setting in which the drinking takes place and the expectancies that lie behind the experience. The age of the drinker is also a factor. A thirty-five-year-old patient in our clinic told me that after he had had three or four highballs, he experienced a remarkable sense of buoyancy and an intense desire for adventure. At such a stage in a drinking evening, he would go out on the town, join up with strangers or telephone many of his girl friends until he found one whom he could go to visit or who might consent to go out with him. This patient was shy and sexually fearful when sober, and although his performance both in human relations generally, and in sexual relations particularly, deteriorated when he drank heavily, his motivation and desire for such experience seemed to increase. I remember another patient, sixty-five years old, who was in the hospital at the same time who said that for him the most attractive thing about drinking was to make himself comfortable all by himself, at home if possible, and if not at home, in some hotel room where he could drink quietly and steadily for a whole evening, becoming gradually more peaceful and sedated until he fell into a stuporous sleep. Unfortunately, such sleep would last only three or four hours for him and he would awaken quite suddenly, fully alert, nervous, anxious, and tremulous, with an intolerable need to drink himself into a coma again.

The effects of alcohol upon the nervous system are indeed a matter of serious concern, and they constitute a principal reason why alcohol, when used as a beverage, may become a problem. However, alcohol may also affect other organs and systems of the body. For example, the use of alcohol, particularly in high concentrations, can bring about local irritation and inflammation of the stomach wall, giving rise to the gastritis and "indigestion" that some people have after drinking. As is well known, alcohol acts as a diuretic, that is to say, there is an actual increase in kidney activity with enhanced urine production. This is probably caused by a direct effect of alcohol upon the pituitary gland which, in turn, among its many functions, regulates kidney secretion. Alcohol probably acts upon the pituitary gland like a stressful stimulus, and since the pituitary is a regulator of all endocrine glands, it is not surprising that drinking alcohol, especially in large amounts, can disturb endocrine functions (such as sexual activity).

The liver has a necessary role in burning alcohol in the body, and while a healthy liver can handle this function when moderate amounts of alcohol are involved, it will not do so when seriously damaged by heavy drinking. A few drinks also cause the heart to beat somewhat faster and the blood vessels of the skin to dilate or enlarge. The output of blood from the heart is dimished, and new studies show that heart muscle becomes damaged by alcohol.

As we have seen, there is a sense of warmth from drinking, but the dilatation is actually a cause of increased loss of heat from the body so that drinking before exposure to cold is not beneficial. In times past more than at present, alcohol has been used as a medicine. For example, patients who have had a coronary attack have sometimes been given alcohol in the diet on the theory that it dilates the coronary vessels (the arteries supplying heart muscle) and so improves the blood supply to the heart. Alcohol actually has no such action upon heart vessels. The main medicinal value of alcohol is for older people in whom it acts in moderate amounts as a mild tranquilizer, promoting sleep, relieving aches, pains, and irritability, and stimulating appetite. For most other purposes alcohol has been supplanted by better medications. In short, drinking has no beneficial effect on human health and may be detrimental in the long run.

PART II
The Causes of Problem Drinking

4
Motives for Drinking or Abstaining

There are three general patterns of drinking which it is appropriate to examine at this point along with the motivational drives that lie behind them. These three patterns are the traditional social pattern, the contemporary social pattern, and the various patterns of individual drinking. Before we begin this examination, we should note that we cannot be certain that these social patterns will continue to prevail among young adults who are now in their twenties. The basis for this statement is twofold: the determination of young people to set their own patterns; and the impulsiveness with which they deal with alcohol and other drug problems.

Traditional Motivations

Traditional cultural patterns of drinking are not often analyzed in a clear-cut, conscious way by those experiencing them, nor are the motivational factors always understood. Yet these patterns make a strong impression on the members of a cultural community and usually have a deep and abiding influence. The fact that they may be unexamined deprives these patterns of not one whit of their social strength, because they are usually followed in a natural way by the participating member of the group at an early age within the family setting. Traditional patterns of social drinking provide a loosening of the bonds of strict self-control in a controlled situation. And while they allow for celebration, cheer, and relaxation, they also set clearly the limits within which this is to take place. They both allow the use of alcohol and protect the user from misuse. Thus what is acceptable behavior is not only clearly defined but also has the firm support of the cultural unit.

These patterns are followed by the individual in the traditional settings of special occasions: births, baptisms, weddings, and funerals. Later there may be other occasions such as holidays, farewells, and reunions. Since we derive a sense of continuity and security from family and cultural traditions, the imprint of these traditional patterns stays with us. The validity of this is attested by familes and cultures that still practice ritual drinking, the Italians and the Jews, for example. Their traditional patterns will remain so long as the family and cultural community remains intact.

American society, however, is a mobile society. Extended families no longer live in close geographical proximity. Individuals, together with their families, are forced for one reason or another to move frequently, so that neither the extended family nor religious or ethnic groups maintains their cohesiveness. When this happens, members of these groups may, after some confusion or disorientation, attempt to adopt the patterns of drinking within their new communities or associations; and the traditional habits of the former groups are dimmed or lost completely. This situation is commonplace among second- and third-generation families of immigrants who originally brought with them to this country valuable traditions and restraints with respect to the use of alcoholic beverages. All of us are part of the ongoing traditions of our families, communities, and culture. We depend upon the culture, and are strengthened and supported by the activities which the culture provides and which assure us that we belong to an enduring and orderly tradition. We should, therefore, intelligently appraise the traditions that we have inherited in order to decide what is of value and should be perpetuated, and what to abandon as inappropriate and archaic. In specific relation to drinking, it is, I think, as important to respect the tradition of abstinence among some of our neighbors as it is to appreciate the traditional cultural patterns of drinking among others.

The Contemporary Pattern of Social Drinking

The rationale for the pattern of social drinking which is widely practiced today might be stated as follows: The use of alcoholic beverages in company is an adult privilege to be used with discrimination and good taste. Such use is part of cultivated and civilized life and one of the joys of gracious living. Thus these beverages are a prominent feature of the "candlelight and silver" atmosphere of a successful and attractive life. In fact, the ability to provide one's guests with quality beverages is an accepted symbol of success and prestige. In the business world the serving of alcoholic beverages is an accepted feature of both negotiating and entertaining.

One or another of these points is frequently stressed by commercial advertisers. They present us pictures of the elegant dinner or wedding party, the prestigious banquet, the gracious cocktail hour, where the association is with interesting, successful, brilliant people and where the combination of relaxation, good company, and joyful associations prevail. Advertisers also exploit the gourmet—it is a mark of cultural distinction to be knowledgeable and discerning about vintage wines, fine brandies, and liqueurs, specially blended and aged spirits. All these attributes—gracious living, prestige, gourmet taste—have a strong and growing appeal for Americans today.

Drinking in the settings we have described is frequently referred to as social drinking. The people involved feel that they are rewarded by alcoholic consumption and their image enhanced by it. Since their savoir-faire is acknowledged and appreciated by their peers, their behavior and practice receives immediate reinforcement.

We must, however, examine more carefully the term "social drinking." *Social drinking* is not simply the drinking of host and guests, or of friends in physical proximity to one another. Nor can the term simply be used to designate drinking that is not problem drinking, drinking that appears to go on without disorder. The term *social drinking,* I believe, should be reserved for those group occasions on which the use of alcoholic beverages facilitates *wholesome and rewarding social interrelations.*

The importance of this definition is that few people normally drink alone. True, a person in a strange city might go by himself to a cocktail lounge for a drink before dinner. Usually, however, drinking is a social practice, and although in the case of the person in a strange city the drink that he has by himself might be comforting, it certainly would not carry with it any social reward. When two or more people have drinks together, the drinking is only to be called social when they become more attractive, pleasant companions and their relationship is fostered. The fact that one member of the group feels more relaxed or more content with himself does not necessarily make the drinking of the group social. It is necessary that the *group* who are drinking together not only feel more relaxed and contented, but that they are socially better people for it. In other words, a primary function of the drinking is to cement friendship, and to improve understanding and good relationships. The drinking in itself is always secondary to the social objectives. When the drinking becomes the main purpose of the occasion, the practice can hardly be termed "social drinking," since it has now come to serve needs of a different character.

It is unfortunately true that at certain gatherings, such as a cocktail party, the evening may begin with what can be called social drinking. As the evening proceeds, however, the social relationships can become more and more tenuous and threatened, and the isolation of one person from another begins as heavy drinking blocks communication and dissolves relationships. At such times, the psychological, as well as the physical, noise level interferes with what people are trying to say and to be to each other. The wholesome objectives of social drinking are lost sight of by the group.

Motivations for Individual Drinking

Our discussion of what can happen at a cocktail party when it ceases to fulfill the definition of social drinking leads naturally to a consideration of the patterns of individual drinking, or what some call psychological drinking. The motivation for these patterns can vary widely, but they share in common a psychological framework. The two most common patterns are the following:

Drinking mainly to relieve anxiety and tension: In the early phases of drinking, the individual usually entertains the hope that his anxieties and tensions will be effectively relieved by a drink or two. This is generally true of most people who, after a hard day's work, frankly seek to relax and unwind by having drinks before dinner and, perhaps, a liqueur after dinner. Many American homes—the parents and sometimes the elder children as well—follow such a pattern. These families may be by no means alcoholics, yet they have this need to be "tranquilized" before dinner. And as our culture is structured and functioning today, alcohol is the most popular tranquilizing substance in use.

The reasons for using alcoholic beverages in the hope of a tranquilizing effect are not hard to understand. On the job many people are compulsive, conformist, and subservient. They fear that they may lose their jobs almost any time, or they are tormented by their failure to advance in rank. They see our society as fiercely competitive; and they regard American industry (and they are probably partly correct in this) as a cut-throat operation in which the devil takes the hindmost. They have lost confidence in Government. The evening drink is a temporary holiday from the day's striving. Others simply apply themselves diligently to their jobs from Monday through Friday and then experience a lost weekend of heavy drinking.

Two observations are in order here. First, tension can be healthy in tolerable amounts under appropriate circumstances, and one should learn how to face tensions and deal with them in other ways than along the pharmacological route. Second, some patterns of drinking, not necessarily to be classified as alcoholism, not only fail to relieve tension but often increase it, because there is a kind of "kickback" from drinking that may come later in the evening when the day's troubles rush back in after the effects of the drinking have worn off. It must always be remembered that alcohol as a tranquilizer is by no means an ideal medication for people whose worries and tensions are abnormal. There is truth in the statement, "If you really need a drink, it is not good for you." For whenever alcohol is used as a drug for potent effects, it is dangerous. Alcoholic beverages are not adequate for the function of blotting out serious and difficult problems; at its best, alcohol should be a social beverage used for mild effects.

Drinking to escape boredom: This is often stated as a motivation by alcoholics and other problem drinkers as well as by those who do not see their use of alcohol as a problem. Boredom and inertia inevitably attack people from time to time. But those who are driven by compulsive work habits or are overworked find themselves in their free time suffering from intolerable ennui and boredom with which they cannot cope. In such cases a drug-regulated life is not uncommon. A patient who worked twelve or more hours a day informed me that on rising at four-thirty in the morning, he took amphetamines to get himself started. During the day he would drink whiskey to keep going; toward evening or even during supper he would fall asleep, but by bedtime at eleven he would be unable to sleep and had to take barbiturates. For anyone caught up in this pattern, the world can really seem meaningless, especially when it is mechanized and depersonalized. The weekend, particularly, is a time of intolerable loss of drive, and drinking seems to hold out the only relief. The difficulty with such drinking, however, is that the boredom and aimlessness become progressively worse, and the individual loses his capacity for the excitement of new experiences, of planning for the future, and of the joys of daily achievement. Meaning and purpose recede, and he becomes more and more vulnerable to the false answers to be found in alcohol.

Some Motives for Abstinence

The reasons for abstaining from alcohol are various and well taken, and they should be thoroughly understood. As with the pattern of social drinking, abstinence is for many people a style of life stemming from a family tradition which never included the taking of alcoholic beverages. Others abstain because it is an infallible way of avoiding alcoholism—which cannot be gainsaid.

Total abstinence may indeed be a satisfactory way of life for many, but it is important that total abstainers understand their own motivations and beware the temptation of assuming self-righteously that they are necessarily following a better way.

The example one sets with respect to his drinking or nondrinking is influential on others, and the total abstainer who is unselfconscious and comfortable with his pattern of abstinence sets an excellent example. It is always well to remember that conscientious people differ in their attitudes toward alcohol, and the abstainer is not necessarily committed to crusade for abstinence. For those who do band together to reduce or abolish alcohol use, it is important not only that they be equipped with the best possible scientific, sociological, and psychological facts, but also that they present their position in regular nonpolemic dialogue with those of the opposite view.

Physical and Psychosocial Reasons: Many people abstain from alcohol because they do not like either the taste or effects of alcoholic beverages. There is really no physiological benefit from drinking. Others will take a single drink for sociability on occasion, but they avoid anything beyond that because of a headache and a generally uncomfortable feeling. In other words, they have low tolerance to alcohol as confirmed by their metabolic reaction. Both abstainers and drinkers may also be uneasy with and anxious about the effects of alcohol on other people, for it is not universally true that people are invariably more social when drinking. Any one of these reasons is a proper motive for abstinence.

There are many people who take pleasure in activity and in their being in top-form. They abstain from alcohol because it infringes on that pleasure. They dislike strongly the sluggishness, loss of control, and so forth that accompanies some drinking; and they very wisely abstain.

Some people "work off" their feelings or, in other ways, deal with their psychological problems. Such people tend to be relatively immune to becoming alcoholics; indeed, they are usually conservative about the use of drugs of any kind, although they may have other vulnerabilities. I am not sure that they are necessarily better-adjusted people, for their breaking points may be expressed in other modes of behavior.

Practical Motives: One of the most practical motives is to abstain for reasons of efficiency. There are times when sharp senses, keen judgment, alertness, and normal reflexes are required—and the use of alcohol can endanger performance, with the resulting sluggishness harming not only the person but others. This is particularly true of pilots, surgeons, engineers, and many others whose skill ought not to be jeopardized. Driving a car, for example, is a skilled operation not to be blunted by the use of alcohol.

Of course, abstinence at times can be a matter of health. For example, those who become alcoholics cannot really ever drink again safely even in moderation and a completely alcohol-free way of life is essential. There are other conditions in which alcoholic beverages may also be inadvisable, as in some cases of peptic ulcer. Alcoholic beverages are still prescribed for certain conditions; but as medical science advances and newer drugs appear, the use of alcohol for specific illnesses is becoming relatively rare.

Some people forgo alcohol as they would any luxury not necessary to life and happiness. Alcoholic beverages are expensive, not essential to life, and are classed as extras or luxuries. Some people will abstain as a measure of economy and apply the money saved to more important needs, such as the education of their children. On the other hand, those who have little are often willing to sacrifice some needs in order to enjoy some luxury. Unfortunately alcohol has served this function and become a great evil in the lives of the deprived and impoverished. One can well understand why underprivileged people may turn to alcohol or other drugs to alleviate the drabness and unhappiness of life.

There is statistical evidence, however, that drinking and

other drug problems are now quite widespread and cross economic, educational, and cultural lines; certainly these problems are not confined to any particular age group. The general trend of our times seems to be to so indulge in luxuries that they become necessities. Yet this matter of abstinence from alcoholic beverages when motivated by the intention to forgo a luxury brings up the question whether some scrupulous, overconscientious people may not be better advised to allow themselves at least some modest luxuries. I have had patients—not problem drinkers—who were so conscientious in denying themselves that they eventually found themselves incapable of enjoying harmless pleasures to be found in the modest good things of life.

Abstinence for the Sake of Others: There is a longstanding and quite well-established view that commends the practice of abstinence to help others. It may be practiced to set an example for children or for a spouse with a drinking problem. Wives or husbands of alcoholics often ask whether it would help if they stop drinking for their spouse's sake. It is a mistake to be too ready to accept as a fact that one's own self-discipline will necessarily encourage, support, or uphold someone who cannot drink safely. Alcoholics and, more particularly, members of Alcoholics Anonymous do not necessarily agree that the abstention of nonalcoholics close to them helps with their problem. In fact, some alcoholics react against such abstention in their family as a reproach to them for their conduct. It is, as it were, to say, "Look I am giving up something to help you, and you had better respond to me." In family situations, then, the question of use or abstinence on the part of the nonalcoholic members should be worked out on an individual basis with really loving consideration for all concerned, including the alcoholic member himself. I have encountered situations in families where I felt that abstinence for all was a good thing; on the other hand, I have had many family situations where I felt that it was indeed better for the moderate drinking members to continue their practice, without, however, flaunting it.

One should point out here a third situation which sometimes comes about: where the nonalcoholic member or members of the family "join the alcoholic" in his disability. Wives have reported, "I finally gave up. Since I couldn't stop him from drinking, I started drinking with him." There are not a few alcoholics who have entered into their disorder in this way. For alcoholism is in a sense a communicable disorder, and a person can become "infected" by his alcoholic partner.

The motive to abstain in order to help others has often been reinforced by St. Paul's statement in I Cor. 8:9, "lest our own liberty become a stumbling block to the weak." It is true that a person can indulge in certain behaviors that are innocent enough so far as he is concerned yet are dangerous or non-supportive so far as those around him are concerned. While St. Paul was not primarily speaking of the use of wine in this quotation his caution does apply to drinking. In his letter to the Romans (14:21), at the end of a magnificent discourse on Christian love and differences of conscience, he says "It is right not to eat meat or drink wine or do anything that makes your brother stumble." I find no fault with this at all, particularly as St. Paul makes it clear that we do not belong to ourselves alone and that we do not have liberty or license to act only with ourselves in mind. It is a fact that we belong to God; and if actions that may not trouble us injure others, then we are "no longer walking in love" (Rom. 14:15). It is a solemn misdeed to let our actions cause the ruin of one for whom Christ died. Moreover, St. Paul makes a strong plea for tolerance and reasonableness in questions of conscience, asking those who abstain not to pass judgment on those who do not and for those who do not abstain to be equally careful not to despise those who do.

Abstinence as a Religious Discipline: An important aspect of the worship of God is to give up something, not because it is evil or wrong, but because by such denial one may better serve and love God. This kind of discipline has authentic religious value for many people. All of us deny ourselves something in one way or another as part of an orderly pattern of life. A medical student, for example, must deny himself many pleasures and recreations during his years of training. Self-denial is an acceptable practice when it is directed toward a meaningful goal. It can, however, subject those practicing it to false pride; and when practiced excessively it can impoverish personality and induce a certain self-centeredness. Many of us know so-called "self-made men" who have over the years lost much of what makes life satisfying.

Americans indulge themselves freely, and yet they are often inclined to view the drinking behavior of the alcoholic as an expression of gluttony. When a nonalcoholic overdrinks, his drunkenness is properly spoken of as the sin of gluttony. The behavior of the alcoholic, however, is in a different moral and ethical category from that of the nonalcoholic. [Ford (2)] Not that the alcoholic is without responsibility in the matter of his drinking, for he has a moral imperative to avail himself of treatment to correct his condition. This differentiation between the drunkenness of a nonalcoholic and the drunken behavior of an alcoholic should be made clear. Our failure to grasp the distinction can blind us to the moral and ethical issues. Alcoholics, like anyone else, should review their own behavior, and they have the ethical responsibility to do so as one can learn by following the A.A. twelve steps. The drunkenness of the nonalcoholic is a different matter—a form of gluttony. Some believe that one of the best ways to reduce and even elminate problem drinking is to promote the attitude, particularly among young people, that drunkennesss is unacceptable, irresponsible behavior. Even nonalcoholics should have help in avoiding drunkenness.

We all ought to remind ourselves that all we have, we received as gifts from God. We should, therefore, use any of God's "gifts and creatures" with grateful thanks. If one cannot thank God for one's alcoholic drink, one ought not to drink it. It is a great pity that some people, religious or otherwise, who drink only occasionally or moderately, do so with the sneaking feeling that they are doing wrong. Any person who makes a mature decision to drink moderately and with responsibility with due regard to the feelings, needs, and safety of others should do so with thanksgiving to God. If he finds that he cannot do this with a good conscience, he should reexamine his motives and practices, and perhaps seek counsel of those who are trained in the field of alcohol problems.

Abstinence, Clergymen, and Other Professionals: Is it right for a layman to drink but wrong for a clergyman to use alcoholic beverages? There can be, as stated, professional reasons for temporary or enduring abstinence. More and more it is now felt that the clergyman is under the same responsibility as others for making intelligent and wise decisions about his drinking or nondrinking practices. Sometimes clergymen will drink with their parishioners because they think that this may make the parishioners feel that they, the clergymen, are closer to them or "good fellows." I think this is an immature motivation for drinking. I believe that a clergyman who belongs to a church that interdicts drinking for the clergy should keep the promises he has made; if he objects to them, he should work for their repeal. There are times and occasions when a drink is inimical to a clergyman's performance of duty, just as in the case of a physician or a surgeon. Unfortunately, there are clergy who drink for these immature reasons, and not a few of these do fall victim to drinking problems, or even alcoholism.

There is an unfortunate, but apparently inevitable, tendency to brand professional people who are alcoholics with a stigma. In view of this fact, special treatment facilities for clergymen and other professionals have been established, and the best of these facilities have good records of helping their patients. At the present time, however, the policy of receiving and treating the professional person who is alcoholic just as anyone else in a similar milieu is gaining ground.

I have had many alcoholic patients who are clergymen, doctors, pharmacists or nurses. Generally, they have done very well. Because their problems are sometimes associated with notably scandalous conduct, clergymen in particular unfairly experience great difficulty in returning to their ministry. One clergyman patient was deposed from the ministry by his superiors and divorced by his wife; and even though he achieved sobriety, he was desperately unhappy as an insurance salesman. His death a few years later brought to an end a life that had always been plagued by emotional deprivation and the consequent inability to experience joy.

The point about abstinence or temperance as a religious discipline is that it should be guided by principles of freedom and joy. One can practice temperance through total abstinence or moderate responsible use. If the latter is the choice, it can be successful only if one is able to give thanks to God joyfully—the joy expressed in Psalm 104: "Bless the Lord, O my soul! O Lord my God, thou art very great. . . . thou dost cause . . . plants for man to cultivate that he may bring forth food from the earth and wine to gladden the heart of man. . . . praise the Lord!"

5
The Causes of
Problem Drinking

The line between problem drinking and alcoholism is sometimes hard to distinguish. The Cooperative Commission on the Study of Alcoholism (Plaut [4]) has defined *problem drinking* as the repetitive use of beverage alcohol causing physical, psychological, or social harm to the drinker and to others. Thus it is a rather broad term and includes *alcoholism* which the Commission defined as a condition in which an individual has lost control over his alcohol intake in the sense that he is consistently unable to refrain from drinking or to stop drinking before getting intoxicated. While alcoholism is thus defined as a form of problem drinking, it is not clear why some kinds of problem drinking do not develop into alcoholism within the meaning of the Commission's definition. Thus alcoholism implies problem drinking complicated by a consistent loss of control. In other words, in alcoholism there is an unmistakable addictive feature.

Some General Observations

We should be deeply concerned about problem drinking short of alcoholism because it is in itself a source of ill health and unhappiness. To be able to prevent problem drinking or to initiate early treatment of certain forms of it would greatly alleviate the general alcohol problem.

The following account of a patient's use of alcohol will illustrate concretely what we have been saying about the distinction between problem drinking and alcoholism. This man was a brilliant and successful law professor in a distinguished university who entertained lavishly and, on such occasions, drank freely with his guests. He followed this pattern without obvious harm to anyone for five or six years. At that time he began to have drinks with his lunch. Although he continued a full workday, it was quite obvious that in the afternoon he was less than efficient in his teaching. Gradually, a series of unhappy and unfortunate incidents occurred. He wrecked his car, and his license was revoked. There was also some deterioration of his health. Nevertheless, he maintained fairly well intact his excellent memory and vivid personality, and for some years there was no evidence that he was addicted in the sense that he was unable to stop drinking before getting intoxicated. There were even times when he would go for prolonged periods without seeming to be intoxicated although he was drinking quite heavily. After about fifteen years of problem drinking, for which there had been no specific treatment, alcoholism caught up with him. He finally died with complications of liver cirrhosis and severe brain damage.

Other patients of mine have had a clinical course similar to this one, short of the terminal phases. Many began with what they considered to be normal drinking at about their middle or late twenties. They found they could support their alcohol use quite well; in fact they felt that they could drink with more control than their friends and relatives, and their use of alcohol meant a great deal to them. On the job they were able to meet the necessary mental and physical demands without showing any marked way-signs of their heavy drinking. Around the age of forty, however, there gradually began a subtle and insidious change—they found themselves unable to control their drinking.

One of the difficulties of identifying problem drinkers early is their failure to seek professional guidance in the initial stages of their illness so that their problem is not recognized for what it is. Even when the person has a serious motor accident or is arrested for speeding under the influence, he or she does not necessarily seek or receive professional guidance. Or a person may not consider his drinking a problem because he knows others who drink heavily and harmfully, but have not become alcoholics and seem to live long lives, despite the harm that they do to themselves.

It must also be admitted that physicians and other health professionals are not always quite sure what to do about a problem drinker who does not present clear symptoms of addictive alcoholism, for there is a type of problem drinker who seems to get along reasonably well. What kind of help should be offered in the early or prodromal phases of alcoholism? Should the person be advised to cut down on his alcohol use, or should total abstinence from alcohol be enforced or encouraged? These questions can be answered only after consideration of the individual case. Certainly any person who causes harm physiologically, psychologically, or socially to himself or others should have the benefit of a thorough professional study. A noticeable deterioration in a person's capacity to handle alcohol is an ominous sign. Often such problem drinkers are capable, highly productive people, valuable in their community; they should not be lost.

The Indulgence Theory

One theory of alcoholism that deserves discussion here, because it is so widespread, is that alcoholism and problem drinking are simply self-imposed, habitual indulgence; hence the label *indulgence theory*. Most see this theory as archaic; they are convinced that there must be more to the problem than simple indulgence. The theory, however, has wide appeal; problem drinkers and alcoholics act as if they believed it, as if they want to accept it as an explanation of the way it all began. Unfortunately, it offers no motivation for recovery and simply serves as a barrier to recovery by bogging victims down in their own guilt and paralyzing rehabilitation.

It is my contention that there is no real evidence to support the theory, for there are many indulgent drinkers who never become alcoholics or problem drinkers, while others whose drinking shows no characteristics of self-indulgence become seriously addicted. The behavior of problem drinkers encourages at times the notion that an alcoholic could really stop his drinking if he would sufficiently mobilize his "will power." This oversimplified therapeutic theory has done much to mislead families of alcoholics and to discourage the victims themselves. Feelings of blame and hostility are generated toward the drinker; the situation is worsened; the drinker's remorse often blocks therapeutic progress.

The question of the blame to be associated with or charged against the problem drinker or alcoholic, either by himself or others, is one deserving careful thought, since how the drinker perceives the moral problem may profoundly affect his attitude toward his own recovery. To begin with, we must acknowledge that no pat answer can be given to this question. Problem drinking and alcoholism usually develop in stages, and in framing an answer, we would have first to identify the stage. Then again, if we accept the alcoholic as a person who is ill, then certainly his behavior in an advanced stage is not subject to judgment on the basis of ordinary ethical norms. The question then becomes one of fixing his moral culpability in the course of his becoming an alcoholic. But how important is it at the later stage to try to establish earlier culpability, when the really important issue for the problem drinker or alcoholic is that he accept and bear responsibility for his recovery. This latter I believe to be an unquestioned responsibility. For drinkers struggling with problems of recovery and attempting to meet their responsibility for recovery, their prior blame is irrelevant; and capable therapists tend to accept this resolution of the issue.

Then, too, the indulgence theory, when accepted, has an important bearing on treatment techniques. Therapeutic concern, for example, may be almost exclusively directed toward maintaining abstinence through a Spartan and painful rejection of alcohol at all costs. The patient is subjected to a *battle with the bottle*. If he fails, his therapist and/or his family, friends, or employer will swoop down on him with accusations of failure and of the disgrace that he is bringing upon himself and them. On the other hand, we should note, when this theory does not determine treatment, a therapist is free to consider the person himself, his family setting, his job, and indeed all the aspects of his life. Abstinence, while essential, will not be the only goal although it will be a primary consideration out of which all other rehabilitative procedures will emerge. An occasional slip is not, then, to be regarded as evidence of total failure, but as an experience from which the patient may learn and progress.

Problem Drinking as a Disease

Another approach and theory is summarized in the slogan "Alcoholism (or problem drinking) is a disease; an alcoholic is a sick person who needs and deserves help." This slogan, the focus of considerable controversial discussion, has not found any single, unqualified verification (Jellinek [3, 5]).

Obviously, a problem drinker is manifestly sick when suffering from symptoms of alcohol intoxication or withdrawal. Moreover, the so-called "diseases" of alcoholism such as peripheral neuropathy, cirrhosis of the liver and Korsakoff's psychosis are evidence that disease and illness are involved. Furthermore, an alcoholic's nervousness, his dependency, impulsivity, immaturity, and frequent poor judgment seem to confirm that even when sober (perhaps, especially when sober) he is unwell psychologically. Even so, it is impossible to define alcoholism or any form of problem drinking in terms of a single cause or etiology having an exclusive, characteristic medical and psychological pathology with a narrowly specified clinical course. But we can draw on our clinical judgment to distinguish between nonalcoholics in general, alcoholics, and problem drinkers; and we have sufficient experience and knowledge to enable us to devise helpful treatment enterprises.

In weighing the theory of alcoholism or problem drinking as a disease, we should consider carefully two questions. The first is: To what extent is alcohol itself a cause of alcoholism? Now we know that there is a complex interaction between the person and the drug and that in some cases the alcohol itself may be more important as the cause of problem drinking than in other cases. Some authorities even contend that the "choice" of alcohol as the means of addiction or problem drinking is entirely a matter of chance or at most only a contingent cause. Until we know a great deal more about the biochemical interaction between the alcohol and the person using it, there is much wisdom in advocating that the problem be approached from the basis of presumed underlying human disturbances and that the alcohol itself not be overemphasized in the total situation. This is true of drug abuse generally. This approach, however, if pushed to the extreme, can lead to a therapeutic philosophy which eliminates any special or specific consideration at all being given to the alcohol or other drug as such.

The second question to be considered is: What weight are we to attribute to psychological factors in assessing problem drinking as an illness? Are these factors an overriding cause? Again, some would answer yes and point to preexistent psychological defects of many sorts. Now we must grant that, whatever the preexisting causes may be, there does emerge with the illness a psychopathology that becomes an integral part of the total illness. The problem drinker or alcoholic does not "drink socially" in the usual sense of the term, but uses the alcohol as if it were a tranquilizing medicine. In such cases the problem would seem to originate in the psychologically disturbed person's finding alcohol to have highly desired psychopharmacological effects. But in such cases an important question is just how the central nervous system, liver, and other systems deal with the large amounts of alcohol taken. The illness, therefore, ought not to be limited to psychological considerations exclusively. Indeed, we may reasonably think of the loss of control in alcoholism and other manifestations of problem drinking as symptomatic of multiple etiological factors and which act in a complex way to bring on the behavioral symptoms.

The Diverse Causes (Hoff [6])

The causes of problem drinking including alcoholism are diverse, and it is a mistake to think that any one cause is exclusively operative in all cases. Most likely, there has been a combination of causes. Although we are unable to attribute any distinct, definitive psychological characteristic to problem drinkers (including alcoholics), we do know that we are dealing with a mixed group of unhappy ill people, many who have early suffered severe affectional deprivation, and in childhood or later have borne unusually heavy stresses. Then too, they often experience difficulty in relating in a friendly way with other human beings. So much so that whether they drink alone or with others, the drinking is usually an expression of their isolation, both physical and psychological. It is as if the drinking were taking the place of affectionate, meaningful relations and empathy with others. This may be a result of their drinking as well as a cause of it. They also may have great difficulty in handling the frustrations, delays, and anxieties of daily life. On the other hand, their needs for immediate gratification and "instant living" are very great. To control impulsivity is difficult for them, as it is for many others. The composite of these characteristics, however, is not limited exclusively to problem drinkers but is to be found quite universally, particularly in people who are psychologically impaired. Thus it would be a mistake in cases of problem drinking to consider the alcohol itself as the only etiological or causative agent. In time, by further study of causative combinations, we may be able to develop valid profiles of the alcoholic or problem drinker as a vulnerable person. Thus we may be able to test the vulnerability by physiological and biochemical, as well as by psychological and other, means.

A tempting theory of etiology is one that begins with the observed fact that some people have an immensely high tolerance of alcohol early in their teen years or twenties. Such people rarely have hangovers and seem able to experience safely the profound psychological effects of large amounts of alcohol; they use alcohol freely as a psychological drug rather than develop a normal growth and maturity. When alcohol tolerance breaks down at about forty or fifty years of age, such persons are left bereft; they can no longer stand a substance for which they have built a life-long need.

The Prealcoholic Personality: There is a possibility that such a personality type exists, although we are not able at the present time to draw an exclusively characteristic psychological picture. Many psychologists, psychiatrists, and other professionals have reported certain psychological characteristics that seem to be marks often present in problem drinking and alcoholism—such as sexual immaturity. They also cite the inadequacy of problem drinkers for coping with anxiety, frustration, pain, and other undesired experiences or feelings.

One possibly important characteristic is the undue reliance of alcoholics upon environmental fields. While nonalcoholics in the face of conflicting stimuli in an experimental situation will rely more upon proprioceptive stimulation (internally orienting body signals), alcoholics tend to respond preferentially to sensory stimulation from the visual field. Thus it has been said that alcoholics are *field-dependent* people and particularly *visually* field-dependent (Witkin, Karp and Goodenough [7]). It would appear that this is quite likely a prealcoholic characteristic of these patients rather than an outcome of illness. Obviously, further work in this promising area is needed, but it may be hypothesized that at least in some alcoholics disturbances during the first few years of life may have interfered with the development of reliance upon their proprioceptive (internally orienting) system. It is as if the alcoholic, unable to take confidence in his own internal body signals, is constantly, even frantically scanning his external world, much as a search light in a lighthouse does the external environment. His anxieties stem in part from his constant need to explore the outside world and to make sure that it is in order. But since this is an impossible task, he finds himself beset with intolerable anxiety and tension.

This may be the reason why many alcoholics have a low tolerance for tension. Whatever the cause of the tension may be, it seems that some psychological and/or physiological causes of low tolerance are operating, such as *hormonal dis-*

turbances. For example, even relatively small excess of adrenalin-like substances, technically called *catecholamines,* in the system may have a tremendous impact and can lower in a marked way the level of tension tolerance. In our own work in our laboratories, we have found that the cerebral cortex and other higher levels of the central nervous system exercise a significant jurisdiction over the so-called autonomic functions, including the functions of the endocrine glands, the heart, the circulation, and the visceral organs. Such research has begun to give us a rather clear-cut picture of why it is that some people are so nervous and so easily overwhelmed by tension and anxiety. The psychosomatic symptoms often associated with anxiety and tension may stem from unusually sensitive responses of the upper levels of the central nervous system. Thus, for example, we find that stimulation of the upper levels of the brain mobilizes adrenalin activity. This mobilization is certainly a part of the anxiety-tension response, and the mobilizing action can be sedated by alcohol and certain other drugs [Hoff (8)].

Indeed, alcohol is one of the most potent drugs in temporarily reducing the activity of these cortical autonomic activating systems. The unfortunate difficulty is that when the effects of alcohol wear off, the autonomic overaction becomes even greater than it was before. In other words, there is a kind of withdrawal backlash or overresponse; and it is this withdrawal overresponse that is so distressful to alcoholics. They feel powerless to do anything about it: their only recourse is to drink more with temporary relief followed by a further increase of nervousness, tremor, and even convulsions or delirium tremens. It is a terribly depressing experience to find that the pleasure becomes less and less and the problems greater and greater. The depression which they experience is further aggravated by the fact that their friends and family become more and more critical of their behavior and less and less able to understand what is happening.

Alcoholics suffer depression perhaps most of all when they are in a period of acute withdrawal from alcohol. This is one of the most terrifying experiences an alcoholic has to go through. He is afraid to stop drinking out of fear that he may be attacked by seizures or by delirium tremens. He knows that he can usually be relieved within a few minutes by drinking more. He only stops when he becomes so sick that it is impossible for him to continue drinking. The depression of alcoholics, while characteristic, is not exclusively limited to these causes; part of it stems from the dire situation they clearly or vaguely see themselves in. Or alcoholics may suffer some loss, or threat of loss; their depression may arise from attempts to handle the loss by blaming themselves or others or by a variety of anxiety-producing devices.

Because of the conditions we have described, many alcoholics suffer from an intolerance of the present. The reality of the immediate moment is insufferable. The alcoholic often finds unbearable *this sensitive leading-edge of existence*—that interface between the past and the future in which all of us human beings must try to learn to live; and so he seeks to escape from its pains and its decisions and to retreat into temporary self-oblivion. Whatever the cause of the alcoholic's psychological problems, whatever the etiology of his depression, whatever the factors that have brought him to his present psychological dilemma, he is caught up in a situation, as he sees it, which can be relieved only by the chemical comfort that alcohol temporarily gives him. All alcoholics have a secret fear that alcohol sooner or later will let them down, and indeed, most of them are aware of the fact that their relief is not perfect. Even in the depths of the drinking experience, the comfort is less than complete and there still lingers a haunting continuum of fear, anxiety, and unhappiness. The effects of alcohol for the alcoholic are never, therefore, quite perfect but unfortunately, for many of them, this is the only way in which they can find a kind of counterfeit happiness. This is why alcoholism has been described as a spurious way of life from which the victim has no known means of escape. Alcohol is the center around which life revolves; it is all that holds him together; it is all that has meaning for him. He will surrender almost anything to support this way of life, and in this sense many an alcoholic has found in his alcoholism a kind of diabolical chemical religion. Thus, we can grasp why it is that alcoholics can never be really joyous outside of true sobriety.

A variety of childhood experiences has been specified as having psychological consequences that may lead to alcoholism. Early social and emotional deprivation is one frequently reported experience, especially in girls. Indeed, alcoholism in women seems almost to be a special disorder. I have been working successfully for some time with a patient, a young woman of about thirty-two, who cannot remember her father or her mother ever hugging or kissing her or showing any warmth toward her. Her grandmother, who was kind to her, died when she was young, and her grief over this death was unrelieved as she grew older. Thus this patient was ready to do almost anything to win affection. It is not surprising that she became sexually promiscuous although she was almost completely unable to enjoy sexual relationships. Her sexual experiences were both homosexual and heterosexual, neither bringing her satisfaction—the loving tenderness she craved. Her use of alcohol and other drugs became fantastically varied in her search to satisfy this craving.

Then there was another patient who had her first drink when she was about nineteen years old. In childhood she had been sexually attacked by her father, and life for her had become an enigma. She felt alone, unwanted, unclean. At a party she went to in college, she was offered martinis and, after two or three of these, she says that for the first time in her life she felt that her life had meaning. It was as if a miracle had happened to her: her pain was assuaged, the terror of living obliterated temporarily. From that time on, she always used alcohol to handle any kind of frightening or distressful experience. Later in life she prostituted herself, never married, and finally died in her late forties. This patient did find peace and contentment toward the end of her life despite her psychological maiming: through therapy she arrested her drinking and did find joy both in the church and in a growing ability to relate to others.

Alcoholics, by and large, are notably unable or inept in feeling for and relating to others effectively—a failure of empathic perception. Their illness seems to stem from a wide variety of deep-seated psychological problems and personality disturbances. The difficulty in adapting this knowledge to an etiological theory, however, is that many persons with similar psychological disabilities do not become alcoholics or do not become addicted to other drugs. All the same, alcoholism has been called the "lonely disease." I have often thought there are few human beings in this world with so keen a sense of being lost as an alcoholic. This is one reason why their enjoyment of simple natural pleasures is so impoverished and why they so frequently see themselves as victims of boredom, apathy, and the tedium of life.

Then, too, an alcoholic often behaves as if he spent a great deal of his time in guilty brooding on the past, fearing and dreading the future, while being completely unable to tolerate the present. All human beings have existential problems. For an alcoholic, these problems have a particular horror: life is not worth living, and death is preferable to life as he conceptualizes it. This is one reason why it is so futile to suggest to an alcoholic that he stop drinking because he is destroying his life or maybe his liver or his brain. He has already concluded that life is not really worth living. An alcoholic is not likely to arrest his illness simply because progressive deterioration of mind and body threatens, although this is sometimes a motivating factor. Something more is needed; he must begin to accept his life as really precious and worth saving in an eternal sense. Therefore, the essential therapeutic venture becomes one of helping an alcoholic to find reliance on affection and human concern that for some reason he may never have had before.

One of the strategies in reducing problem drinking in any culture is to promote in the culture and in the society, by whatever effective means available, the concept that drunkenness is not merely unacceptable but, more important, unrewarding. The research sociologist is in a particularly favorable position at this time to study the relationship of alcohol and other drug abuse to socio-cultural characteristics and practices. We also stand in great need of more reliable direct methods of measuring the prevalence of problem drinking. One drawback in research on alcohol problems has been a lack of reliable information as to how many alcoholics there are, of whatever kind, and in what segments of society they are to be found. We also lack adequate information on the various clinical courses of alcoholism and of the precise phases of the clinical course at which alcoholics are most likely to respond to rehabilitative intervention.

We shall have occasion to refer later to the relation of family life to emotional disorders and the vulnerability to alcoholism. Here we shall simply state in passing that the family is a vastly important cultural unit, the health of which seems essential for a vigorous society. The society of the family, the society of the community, and the society of the nation are interrelated. The etiologies of problem drinking are without question intimately tied up with family, community, and national pathologies. It is most likely true that very few people become alcoholics or addicted to other drugs simply on their own. These disorders can be described as communicable illnesses that spread in the family, in the community, and in the nation.

To oversimplify, people who become alcoholics are often alienated persons for whom warm human interrelationships have become impossible. Anyone who observes both the overt and suppressed violence and other public sins of our times knows how confused, irritable, hard, and unloving we as a people can become; how our compassion and confidence have dwindled; and how young and old alike are at war with one another. We are critical, we are harsh, we compete unfairly, we are dishonest; and our concern for others is often quite minimal. Despite our protestation of altruism, we are very selective in matters of human concern. In fact, our concern is often so puny that we turn the other way rather than come to the aid of people in sorrow, trouble, need, or danger. Therefore, it is not surprising that we as individuals tend more and more to focus our concerns inward.

I talked last summer with an attractive young man who had a commendable gift for honesty. He confessed that he often found himself severely limiting his relations with others because close relations had become "too painful." This admission is an indictment of the way we are living, yet it is difficult to place blame because we live under perhaps the most bizarre stresses any culture has been called upon to endure. It is common enough, I realize, for intelligent, knowledgeable people to say that the endurance of every age has been severely tested. But what makes the present age so insufferable is that we have at our disposal the abundant means to relieve suffering and promote justice accompanied by the means for total self-destruction. We have the capacity to practice love and to share with others, as well as the opportunity to foster human dignity and the welfare of mankind. Yet our hardness of heart stands out in glaring contrast. Addiction, neuroses, psychopathology have become private, isolated expressions of despair. The fact, however, remains that our best way of preventing alcohol and other drug problems is to try with all our hearts and with our best minds to make a better society. We hope that the Church will see its divine commission inextricably linked with this human mission. If the Church does not, it is hard to tell who will. The time is far advanced and it may even be too late already, although we hope there may still be time.

Physiological and Metabolic Causes of Problem Drinking: While further research into both the psychological and socio-cultural factors in alcoholism seem to hold great promise for developing preventive programs, the study of physiological and metabolic factors seems more likely to produce therapeutic advances in treating the condition.

It is noteworthy, as we have said, that some patients in their prealcoholic stage have, and presumably always have had a high tolerence to alcohol and that their entry into the illness is signaled by a reduction of this capacity. In their prealcoholic days, such people notably "drank others under the table." These facts suggest certain experimental designs for research. With more sophisticated techniques than presently available, biochemists and biologists are likely to become increasingly able to identify the subtle abnormal changes in the ways the body deals with alcohol. It may well be that the breakdown of alcohol in the system of the alcoholic is different from that in the prealcoholic or the drinker who has never become an alcoholic or, indeed, in the person who has never drunk at all. Abnormalities in the metabolism of alcohol or its breakdown products may be responsible for the unusually damaging effects of alcohol ingestion in some people and may have a seriously disturbing effect even in the prealcoholic. The central nervous system neurons may be disturbed in bizarre ways, or there may be unusual effects on the transmission of nerve impulses across the synapses in the brain. These complex excitatory-inhibitory effects of alcohol on the nervous system call for much further study. Thus the physiological and bio-chemical investigation of alcohol metabolism and action in al-coholics and nonalcoholics and the possible differences in the two systems is vitally important.

Brain Damage: A rather special physiologico-biochemical factor in the possible etiology of drinking and other drug prob-lems may be brain damage. The term *brain damage* is some-what loosely defined according to who uses the term, and yet such damage may be responsible for the change in tolerance to alcohol suffered by some alcoholics, as well as for the "mem-ory blackouts" and the loss of ability to control alcohol intake. Emotional factors may play a part too. We know that the cen-tral nervous system becomes abnormally overactive after a heavy drinking period when the alcohol has itself been cleared from the body. Although alcohol leaves the body quite soon (in any case within about 24 hours), this does not mean that the effects are over by then. This overactivity of central neu-rons following clearance of alcohol from the blood and tis-sues may result in convulsions and, if the overactivity is great enough, visual and auditory hallucinations. So-called delirium tremens is a complex of acute and rather terrifying symptoms which are based upon brain overactivity, usually following clearance of alcohol from the system or an acute reduction of the alcohol blood level in a very heavy drinker. This may not only be responsible for convulsions, and delirium tremens, but also may affect those areas of the brain which regulate the so-called autonomic nervous system and so exert control over certain forms of visceral and emotional behavior as has been said.

The autonomic nervous system is that part of the nervous system which links up with nerve connections to the viscera (the heart, intestines, endocrine systems, etc.) and controls in an intricate way more or less automatic actions. When the heart beats fast from fear, what has been called into play is a complex response in the central nervous system linked up with the autonomic nervous system which regulates heart activity. Emotional responses are closely related to the autonomic nervous system also, and thus overactivity of the central nervous system following alcohol withdrawal may in part be responsible for the guilt and depression that alcoholics feel, as well as many of their cardiovascular and other visceral disturbances. It is an unfortunate fact, especially for serious problem drinkers, that alcohol as a pharmacological substance is an imperfect blocking agent for some cerebral autonomic over-responses. Animal studies in our laboratories show that it is inferior to many of the newer psychopharmacological agents in protecting from autonomic overactivity.

Endocrine Glands: Alcoholism has also been specifically linked with disturbances of the endocrine glands. Thus, sexual disturbances notable in alcoholics in part (but only in part) stem from damage to the hormones of the reproduction system. Also, in the long history of basic research on alcohol problems, the thyroid and adrenal glands have been implicated and many hormone therapies have been attempted. In general, such therapies have not been startling in their success, nor have studies which were based on the idea that alcoholics had particular and rather specific vitamin needs. Much research on etiology is generated by the theory that there are genetic differences in individuals which do predispose to alcoholism. Such research is of great merit.

Longitudinal Studies: This term applies to research in which the subject, whether human or animal, is tested and studied for prolonged periods of time. Thus much can be learned from a continuing investigation of a group of young people as they move into adult life. Such studies would include physiological and biochemical investigations, psychological testing, psychiatric evaluation and case histories covering family and social relationships. The advantage of such longitudinal studies is, first of all, that one derives data that are unprejudiced by what happens later. In *retrograde* studies, the findings, even the reporting, are influenced by what happened subsequently. One tends to read into the earlier history inferences that might not otherwise be made if the subsequent history were not known. Longitudinal studies are, however, expensive; and in addition to being time consuming, requiring sometimes years to yield information, there is always present the likelihood that after the study has gone on for a few years, certain factors not included for study will begin to show up as having meaning. Then, too, not the least of the difficulties is that the fact that some of the subjects may drop out for one reason or another. Despite these hazards, we need longitudinal studies if we are to identify with precision the etiological pattern of alcoholics and problem drinking.

6
The Clinical Course

Problem drinking passes through various clinically identifiable phases or stages: the *incipient,* the *critical,* and the *chronic* (Jellinek [9]). In this chapter we shall discuss each of these phases. However, we must bear in mind that problem drinkers differ one from the other both in the phaseology and in the progress of their disorder. That is to say, one problem drinker may exhibit only a single characteristic of a given phase while another may manifest most of the characteristics attributed to it. Nevertheless, there are in these composite phaseologies landmarks that do stand out to guide us.

It goes without saying that in this and other chapters we are commonly referring to both men and women.

The Incipient Phase

The reader may ask, "If I drink, is it likely that I will become an alcoholic?" But, as we have seen, probem drinking, including alcoholism, is due to a whole constellation of causes and the actual use of alcohol itself may be in individuals with a certain metabolic and physiological vulnerability. In this case, such people may get into deep trouble right away, either after the first drink or after a few drinking episodes. Some patients say, "I was an alcoholic from the first drink." Where other causes are dominantly operating, there is a tendency on the part of alcoholics and their families not to recognize just what is happening. Yet it is important that the condition be recognized as early as possible. Unfortunately, while we are able to make some rather shrewd predictions about vulnerability, there are no reliable tests yet. But by making available accurate information about alcoholism and its phaseology and by encouraging enlightened public and professional attitudes, there is reason to hope that many problem drinkers will seek aid before their lives are irretrievably damaged. At many clinics, patients are seeking help at younger and younger ages. Often these young people are patients with serious, deep-seated psychological troubles. Therefore, in answer to the reader's question, it is to be hoped that the description of the clinical phaseologies that follow will help him to discover whether he is in danger of becoming victimized by a drinking problem.

One of the early signs of problem drinking is what might be called *occasional relief drinking* or *symptomatic drinking.* That is to say, people find themselves using alcohol more and more to relieve their tensions. There must be millions of people in the United States who daily come home from work almost painfully looking forward to the relief afforded them by a few cocktails. There certainly is a legitimate sense in which use of alcohol for mild relaxation is appropriate and possibly psychologically beneficial. However, the need for this kind of relief drinking can become more and more insistent and constant. At the same time the person may find that his *tolerance* of alcohol is increasing and that the amount of alcohol that he is taking is increasing also. As previously said, some people may have a high tolerance right from the start. In general, a person who finds himself in great need of alcohol as a source of relief should seek professional guidance, especially if he finds himself drinking surreptitiously, that is to say, stopping on the way home for a couple of quickies or going into the kitchen and having one or more by himself and then going back to the cocktail hour in the living room or den.

One of the earliest indications of the incipient or prodromal phase of problem drinking is the so-called *memory blackout*. Blackout is a partial amnesia or an amnesia that is quite complete for its duration. A person drinks at a party and the next day remembers nothing. He recalls going to the party and what he did up until he drank, but the remainder of the evening is a blank. This phenomenon is quite different from that of "passing out," which is a matter of drinking until one loses consciousness. A person experiencing a memory blackout may not show any apparent intoxication at all at the party and when he asks his friends about it the next day, they will reply, "Well, you were a little quiet, but you were doing perfectly all right." He talked with others at the party, he moved about freely, but he cannot remember afterward what happened. He may even have driven his car home. The first terrifying moment in such a situation comes the next day when the person awakens and rushes to the window to see if the car is in the drive. There is no question that memory blackouts account for many accidents fatal both for the driver and for other motorists or pedestrians.

One such experience of memory blackout may not be a particularly critical prealcoholic sign, but recurrences of them become a real danger signal. One cannot say flatly how many blackouts a person can have before he should do something about it; but my own advice would be that anyone who has a blackout at all should seek medical advice from a physician who will take the matter seriously and institute an adequate diagnostic investigation.

A memory blackout is certainly an indication to the neurophysiologist or the neurologist that the brain is being abnormally affected by alcohol. We must also state, however, that many persons go far into the phaseology of problem drinking before having a memory blackout. Therefore, the absence of a history of blackouts cannot in itself be interpreted as an indication that the person is not a problem drinker or even a confirmed alcoholic. It is well to remember also that the experience of the memory blackout differs in some degree from person to person. For example, I know a man who is not an alcoholic and yet who during World War II experienced one or two blackouts at parties. At one of these parties there was a period of about half an hour or a little more of which he retained no memory. He talked with many people at the party and was not, as he discovered later, considered abnormal in his behavior. The rooms where the party was held were warm but not excessively so. His blackout came to an end when he left the party and stepped out into the cold air; and he had no further disturbance of memory that evening. However, he still retained no recall of about a half to three-quarters of an hour at the last part of the party. The frequency of blackouts is important, particularly if they occur after drinking what might be called medium amounts of alcohol. In such circumstances blackouts may indeed foreshadow loss of control and problem drinking of the type which we have designated as alcoholism.

Another characteristic of the early phase of problem drinking preceding loss of control is the practice of sneaking drinks, of having drinks that others do not know about, such as surreptitiously having a stiff drink in the kitchen apart from others at the party. It is as if the person is afraid that there will not be enough and is sensitive about drinking as much as he wants in the company of his wife or his friends. This custom of sneaking drinks may go on throughout all the phases of alcoholism, becoming an even more prominent behavioral characteristic as time goes on, and this sort of behavior seems to indicate that alcohol is beginning to have unusual significance for the drinker, one not shared by the nonproblem drinker.

Very soon the need for taking extra drinks on the side becomes associated with a considerable discomfort or embarrassment on the part of the person when drinking—his own, especially—is discussed. There is preoccupation with the use of alcohol, but the person is sensitive about any references to drinking. This is doubtlessly a protective device: the person does not want his need for alcohol to become known to others or even to himself. It is the opposite characteristic of young drinkers, who, after having been tight or high, make a great thing the next day of their hangover and their intention never to drink again. But the individual who is moving to the prodromal phase of alcohol addiction does not characteristically do this; in fact, the last thing he wants to happen is that knowledge of his need of alcohol become the property of others.

All persons, whether they be problem drinkers, alcoholics, or not, have certain expectations from drinking. That is to say, they look for certain rewards. For nonalcoholics these rewards are presumably mild and do not become serious issues. Those who are moving into or have reached the condition of alocholism have strong needs, and therefore their tendency is to lay greater stress upon the importance of the actual way and manner in which they drink. It is not uncommon in the early phases of problem drinking for a person to take several drinks quickly in rapid succession in order to reach a more comfortable psychological state. Having arrived at this stage of comfort, he may drink rather slowly and continuously in order to maintain this mood which he finds so acceptable. Certainly as the condition of problem drinking advances, the desired behavior is to retain the pleasure of drinking as long as possible so as not to come out of the influence or to go too deeply into it. It is true that some people drink to become unconscious rapidly, but in general I would think that those who drink alcohol as they would take any drug, for the most part wish to have an experience of which they remain aware and which is pleasurable to them. Unfortunately, it is virtually impossible to keep oneself indefinitely at a particular optimum peak or level. What happens—and this is a distressful fact to alcoholics—is that one either comes out of the experience and becomes sick or one suddenly gets very intoxicated and is unable to walk or think straight. This change can happen quite quickly, and for the person who wants to keep himself at a desired level it is unwanted. Of the many unhappy aspects of alcoholism that I have heard from my patients, probably the most upsetting is the fact that one cannot keep one's drinking pleasurable and rewarding and at the same time under control.

There may be many other problems associated with drinking at this phase. Blackouts may become more frequent. There may be an increased number of motor accidents. There may be a reduction in efficiency at work. The family may become sensitized to the person's drinking and object more or less seriously to it. According to our Cooperative Commission definition (4), alcoholism begins when the person has lost control over his alcohol intake in the sense that he becomes consistently unable to keep from drinking or indeed to stop drinking before getting intoxicated. For some people, loss of control means that after drinking even a small quantity of alcohol such as a glass of beer, there is set up a kind of demand which stops only after the person has become intoxicated. This *point of loss of control* is of tremendous importance because from it one dates the alcoholism and the progressive features of such problem drinking.

There are many persons who do not seem to show classic features of loss of control (Jellinek [5]). That is to say, there are some persons who drink steadily all day long and who may consume large quantities of alcohol but who do not seem to get drunk in a classical sense. Also, unfortunately, there are some who find that their control loss is intermittent. I have had many patients tell me (and I believe quite accurately) that there are times when they can drink two or three drinks at a party and do not actually drink any more or become intoxicated. Then, on some other occasion, they may go into a considerable episode with drinking to intoxication that may last for many days. It is not always easy, therefore, for a person to know about his alcoholism, and since his tendency may be to minimize the danger he is moving into, he may find it difficult to acknowledge that control has been lost.

The Critical Phase

The loss of control marks the onset of a severe exacerbation of the behavioral symptoms of problem drinking. The drunkenness of the person is now more and more obvious to others; it may be accompanied by grandiose and aggressive behavior, progressive loss of ability to perform adequately, and withdrawal into one's own self. This crucial phase of addictive drinking may also be associated with writing bad checks and other forms of extravagance while under the influence. Alcoholics often show a tendency to run up large long-distance telephone bills, sometimes even to call strangers. Drinking in this phase may also lead to great euphoria only to be followed the next morning by remorse, depression, and a sense of having been cheated out of what seemed to have been, during the drinking experience, a wonderful sense of personal glorification. The drinking of one patient of mine in this phase became a stimulus to seeking out his women friends and making extravagant promises to them. Alcoholics in this phase are often quite attractive to those of the opposite sex, especially before ethical and moral deterioration has progressed very far. Such early alcoholics make promises of marriage and many other commitments which they sometimes do not even remember when they emerge from the drinking episode.

The remorse that comes on after the episode is over does stem from their distress about their behavior and from the reproof that their families often give them, but it is also in part a neurophysiological symptom due to overactivity of those neural systems in the brain which are associated with emotions. In the early phases of alcoholism, the victim finds himself attempting to provide excuses and to rationalize his behavior. He begins to develop alibi systems to explain why he became drunk. These alibis may become quite complicated: he may blame his work situation or his family relationships; or he may become more and more isolated. He may lose other interests, withdraw from his friends, quit a job to avoid being discharged.

The drinker's relation with his family becomes more and more strained. At the beginning the family tries to function as if nothing were happening, next it finds itself protecting the alcoholic, and finally, in a desperate kind of gesture, trying to give him "therapy." As the illness progresses, the family also begins to protect itself, and there is reorientation of authority relationships within the family and other changes which add to the alcoholic's own sense of failure, despair, frustration, and anger, as well as remorse. He may try to stop drinking altogether or attempt to control his drinking by various unworkable techniques, such as drinking beer and wine instead of spirits; or he may try changing jobs or moving to another part of the country. At the same time he becomes more and more concerned to protect his supply of alcohol, and often there is a running battle between himself and his family, the latter attempting to keep drink away from him. Even so, the alcoholic at this phase is trying to maintain his functioning, and the question he faces is: "How can I drink and still hold my life together?" It is as if his functioning is still the paramount issue, but as time goes on the protection of his drinking behavior takes precedence over other considerations. Nothing, he finds, must interfere with the drinking; and when it does, whether it be his job or social responsibilities, he surrenders them in favor of his drinking. This is the reason why he avoids his family and friends, why he will allow himself to fall into work and financial troubles, and why he finds himself neglecting his meals, his health, and his hobbies and other recreations.

For many problem drinkers, the disorder moves at a more or less rapid pace into much more fulminating behavioral disorders as well as psychophysiological and psychopathological deterioration. Jellinek has spoken of this as the entry into the so-called chronic phase and he sees taking morning drinks, the first bender, and marked ethical disturbance as being signs of this progression. In any case, at this phase, alcohol is used not only as a psychoactive drug but also a neuromuscular sedative. The severity of the addiction at this phase may be indeed expressed by taking drinks in the morning which now are a necessity because of tremors. The person may not even be able to get going in the morning without taking a stiff drink to enable him to shave, get dressed, and tolerate his food. If he has not done so already, the victim may go on weekend or irregular benders or sprees in which he drinks until he becomes sick. Every alcoholic's clinical course from this time on varies from one to the other, and it must always be remembered that alcoholism can be a fatal illness. During these sprees the person may be run over, he may be beaten up and robbed, he may fall frequently. Many alcoholics suffer at this stage, if not before, from head injuries. They are vulnerable to every kind of environmental threat.

The patient, unable to work and having lost his home and family, may then drift into a deteriorated way of life with people like himself or even more impaired. His thinking is disturbed, he suffers often from indefinable fears and anxieties, he becomes unable to take initiative and is more and more withdrawn. His obsessions with drinking may be constant or they may be intermittent. He drinks away his symptoms temporarily only to find them returning with greater and greater force. Somewhere at this point, an alcoholic may find that he has exhausted his alibi systems. Reality becomes so insistent that he admits defeat. This "hitting bottom" has been designated as an experience in which the alcoholic may become, or does become, accessible to help. An alcoholic can be motivated to "hit bottom" much earlier and to seek help long before physical, mental, and emotional deterioration has proceeded so far. To help bring this about is one of the major therapeutic challenges.

The Accompanying Physical Breakdown

We have spoken of some of the physical and emotional disturbances of this often long clinical progression. We have mentioned the memory blackouts, the benders, and the tremors. As we have indicated the alcoholic is vulnerable to all manner of illnesses. He may, for example, die of pneumonia following exposure while drunk in the streets. His eating disturbances and his alcoholic intake may lead to nutritional disorders. The nervous system and the liver especially are two systems most likely to be involved in the alcoholic's problems. The liver disturbances and damage are caused not only by the direct poisoning effect of alcohol taken in large quantities over a prolonged period, but also by the associated nutritional disturbance. Fortunately, if liver damage is not sufficiently profound, there is often considerable restoration for the alcoholic who arrests his drinking. Brain damage carries with it a more grave prognosis, although the liver damage in itself is grave enough. We may diagnose brain damage by clinical examination and also by psychological test procedures which indicate organic brain involvement. Loss of efficiency in work, memory defects, and so forth are some of the indications. At advanced stages of alcoholism, the illness known as Korsakoff's syndrome is one characterized by profound memory disturbances and other symptoms of thought disorder. Depending upon the stage of their illness, alcoholic patients, on entering a hospital or a clinic, will have many things wrong with them. They may have *peripheral neuritis* with pains in their arms and legs and difficulty in walking. Sometimes there are also acute and subchronic disturbances in the cerebellum and other parts of the brain associated with locomotion. With appropriate medical and nutritional treatment, some of these subside in the matter of a few days, weeks or months if the drinking is stopped.

Probably the most dreaded troubles alcoholics suffer from are those of the nervous system: tremors, convulsions, and hallucinations. These combine in what is known as *delirium tremen*s. It is now generally believed that these difficulties are associated with withdrawal from alcohol in a person who has been drinking heavily for many weeks or even in a patient who abruptly cuts down his drinking and so reduces his alcohol blood level. We thus think of these symptoms as *withdrawal* *symptom*s. The tremors are terrifying, and the alcoholic's first impulse is to turn to more drink. This relieves the tremors temporarily. Convulsions also occur in some cases within a few days after arresting a heavy drinking spree unless proper medications are given. Sometimes convulsions and acute psychosis occur within a short time of each other. As I write this, I am thinking of a woman patient of forty-one who came into the hospital last Wednesday. She had been drinking very heavily, about a fifth a day for a number of weeks. On the evening of admission, she had a *grand mal* seizure. When I saw her the next morning, the patient was rational, had minimized her drinking, and felt that she did not belong in the hospital. However, in spite of a sound program of sedation, the patient was irrational and confused on the second day after admission, but was not hallucinating in the sense that she had no visual or auditory symptoms. The patient is improved today. Many alcoholics are terrified to stop drinking because of this fear that they will hallucinate or have seizures; and unfortunately, this is a very real fear. Neurophysiologically, these withdrawal symptoms appear to be caused by an overactivity of systems in the brain which control motor functions and visual and auditory functions.

A real problem is that these terrifying withdrawal symptoms usually contribute nothing toward motivating a patient towards achieving a consistent alcohol-free way of life. This may be partly because memory of the experience is erased within a few days. But a more important reason for the failure of the withdrawal experience to motivate the alcoholic to sobriety is that it is associated in his mind with his attempt to quit drinking rather than with the drinking itself. Such false association is a general problem in the whole course of alcoholism. It provides the basis for an alcoholic's alibi system all along the way. It is only when the alibi system breaks down and the alcoholic finds himself admitting defeat and bankruptcy that he finally is in a position to initiate and continue a program of abstinence and recovery.

It should be said that "hitting bottom," wherever it occurs in the progression, certainly can be a serious and effective motivation for recovery. We do not know, unfortunately, how many alcoholics hit bottom only to destroy themselves in one way or another. To admit that one is powerless over alcohol and that one's life has become unmanageable may simply lead to depression and paralysis of action. On the other hand, however, this can be the beginning of an upward trend. Thiebaut (10) calls the experience of hitting bottom *surrender:* the victim acknowledges defeat. Then, like a person on a runaway horse, through one sort of help or another, he is brought to a sharp halt and turns around in a new direction. Thiebaut calls this turning point *conversion.* Such an experience may be enduring, provided that the alcoholic does not rebuild his alibi system and start drinking again. Therapy becomes a really serious engagement when the patient truly retains his experiences of surrender and conversion. He may have *slips* as they are called; but his actual involvement in therapy is evaluated by the tenacity with which he persists in his surrender experience. While other motivations are valuable in an auxiliary way, the patient's own felt need to recover is certainly the major factor in his recovery. He puts himself and his recovery first; his abstinence becomes a means toward that end.

Somewhere toward the later phases of alcoholism, the tolerance of alcohol noticeably diminishes. Patients describe this by saying, "I get sicker quicker," and in other ways they recognize that the alcohol gives them fewer rewards and causes them more and more sickness. It is as if in acknowledging this, they are putting on one side of the balance the so-called "rewards" of alcohol, but finding on the other side of the balance that they pay an ever greater price in terms of sickness, trouble, and misery. When the patient at last discovers that his drinking is costing him more than it is worth, it now becomes possible for him to travel the road to recovery.

7
The Motivation
to Stop Drinking

Virtually all services providing treatment for problem drinkers attach importance to motivation. It is not proper, however, to assume from this that a correct criterion for evaluating motivation is the patient's simply *wanting* to stop drinking. A few facilities still seem to be interested in working only with patients whom they define as adequately motivated in this respect. I do not think anyone *wants* to stop drinking, particularly a person addicted to alcohol. If there is anything to the phenomenon of "hitting bottom" at all, it is that the victim has finally come to the conclusion that he *has* to stop drinking, whether he wants to or not. Even patients who come to the hospital for treatment on a voluntary basis carry with them into the hospital various qualities of compulsion. In one way or another, they have been forced into a corner by their families, by themselves, or by their employers, and while, with one voice, they will say, "Yes, I must stop drinking," with another voice, they say, "No."

Motivation, then, cannot be regarded as an all-or-none phenomenon. For the motivational factors that lead problem drinkers to seek help are various: it can be to sober up, to achieve a more enduring sobriety, to alter one's life-style, or to change one's self-concept. Moreover, the quality of motivation varies from day to day and often from hour to hour.

Because these patterns vary and shift so, it is unwise for a therapist to say with finality that any given patient is or is not ready for treatment; and certainly it is a great mistake to hold that nothing can be done until a patient decides that he wants to stop drinking. And it is an even greater mistake to suppose that a motivated patient is more worthy of treatment than a non-motivated patient.

Although motivational factors are thus very complex, they can be handled positively. Sometimes the therapist simply has to accept the fact that the patient is not "ready" for therapy, as Alcoholics Anonymous members sometimes do. Sometimes he must accept the fact that the person has not yet reached "bottom" to the extent that he is willing to see therapy as an absolute essential. At such times, the therapist must avoid the temptation of casting undue blame either on the patient or on himself. The truth is that there is no question of blame really involved. Nevertheless, it is a defective attitude to reject for treatment of all problem drinkers who do not fit a ready-made motivational image. As therapists, we approach patients with the best will and with the greatest resourcefulness we have and we should expect the patient to do the same. It is a mistake to dismiss an unfavorable outcome as evidence of the patient's lack of motivation or of our own professional skill or qualifications. On the other hand, there should be regular evaluation of a patient's progress. A change of therapies or therapists may be called for. Indeed, this matter of motivating problem drinkers equally involves motivating staff to accept patients.

We should also observe here that a patient's motivation may often be affected by the cultural environment of the therapeutic services and also by the cultural expectations and limitations of the therapists. Some services are geared to "upper"- or "middle"-class patients, others are geared to so-called lower-class patients. Some techniques of an organization will be effective with one group, but not with another. The essential point, regardless of the group to which patients may belong, is to help them to find a confident, trusting feeling that their problems are considered important and that they themselves are considered worthwhile, valuable people whose lives are precious. Moreover, any treatment program that is to develop motivation effectively must transcend cultural factors and bring out the issues of common humanity upon which all therapy should be based.

Obstacles to Motivation

When problem drinkers and their families understand that not only the therapists but the other care-giving professions in the community are genuinely interested in helping, and that the attitude toward them is not one of condemnation, they are encouraged to seek help openly and intelligently. A fifty-year-old woman patient whom I saw recently has been a very distinguished civil servant in foreign service. She has been all over the world; she is multilingual. She has become a victim of alcoholism and a great part of her difficulty now in seeking help is her shame in having let so many people down. The last thing she needs now is condemnation.

Many of the difficulties from which problem drinkers and their families suffer are problems that have been compounded by neglect. Early entry into therapy might have prevented some of these difficulties, especially if therapy had been undertaken before brain damage or other deterioration occurred.

When therapy begins, one of the chief obstacles is the patient's own lack of clarity about where his problem lies. In the earlier stages of his illness the victim of problem drinking may indeed have been making a valiant effort, not necessarily to stop drinking but to continue to secure what he conceives to be the rewards of his drinking—whatever they may happen to be—in the fervent hope that he will not have to pay too high a price for these rewards in terms of unwanted symptoms, destructive behavior, personal and economic loss, and deterioration. In other words, he has been acting as if it were possible to secure simultaneously both the rewards of drinking and immunity from trouble; and when asked to tell about his experience, he will talk about these efforts. But a problem drinker finds it unpalatable to accept fully the fact that he is becoming or has become unable to handle alcohol and that his life has become or is becoming unmanageable. Actually, the very thought of a regime of complete and endless abstinence holds out a bleak future for him. To face squarely the unpleasant reality that he can no longer support his life situation and still drink, is depressing and intolerable. Hence there are recurrent rationalizations and compromises to postpone rehabilitation or change after therapy has begun. When he finally arrives at the point of accepting his absolute need for treatment because he can no longer cope with alcohol, he has reached a point where he may be available to effective therapy.

At this time, he needs a confident, encouraging therapist whom he can trust. Nevertheless, anything short of this poignantly felt need for help seems to be an inadequate motivation for real recovery. I myself can remember very few patients who I thought arrested their drinking without some kind of strongly experienced sense of need to achieve an alcohol-free way of living for the sake of their own health. I think that many people enter into therapy of a sort without really having this deeply felt need or at least without having expressed it to themselves in clear-cut terms.

The goal of abstinence for a day at a time, is, in my judgment, more helpful than the strong resolve never to drink again; and a patient may be helped to understand that this achievement of day-to-day abstinence is not necessarily easy but it is definitely possible. Sometimes alcoholics fall into the trap of thinking that after a few months, they may be able actually to drink in a controlled fashion. Therapists and care-givers can help a patient greatly by candor as to what they think about the possibility of returning to controlled drinking. We do know that some have asserted that this is possible in a few cases, although I have never seen this verified in an addicted drinker.

An important step in motivating a problem drinker is to help him, in one way or another, to understand that his case involved a multiplex of disorders and disturbances, some physiological, some psychological, some social or spiritual, and some economic. Therefore, the therapist must try to help the patient to want recovery in a broad and deep sense, and to understand that such recovery can be accomplished with skillful help. The patient cannot really do it alone, although as all of us know, cases of so-called spontaneous achievement of abstinence are reported. To become a *recovered* alcoholic is not simply to stay dry; it also involves the reestablishment of relationships and the patient's seeing and coming to grips with some of his most basic problems.

I had several times on my service a woman patient of intelligence and talent. Her trouble had been that as soon as she began to feel a little better, she desired to be discharged; she had followed this practice in all of her contacts with therapy. She hardly ever spent more than two or three days in the hospital, just enough time to get sobered up. Her motivation was to have her immediate discomforts relieved, to feel better, and to get out as quickly as possible. The more all therapists and care-givers become aware that such "therapy" is generally useless, the more successful we shall be. Happily, this patient has now become committed to helping other patients through work in an outpatient clinic. She finds this deeply satisfying and is now achieving continuing sobriety.

General physicians, specialists in various medical disciplines, and counselors in various fields associated with rehabilitation today are asking questions about motivation. It is important for them to do so if there is to be clarity about just how, and with which patients, the most useful therapeutic work can be accomplished. If we do, it may be that we will begin to recognize that a division of labor is in order with some professionals working with certain types of patients, and some with other types.

Motivation must be fostered from the moment of first contact. The worst thing that can happen is for the patient to think that he is being given the "run around." The patient that goes for help and has to wait all afternoon before he is seen, and then is shunted from one person to the other, is going to risk having what motivation he had knocked out of him. It is not surprising that such a patient will say, "This is the way it always is with me. Nobody cares about me. I might just as well give up hope, anyway." Even with the most wholesome interest shown by the therapeutic group, some patients do misinterpret and misevaluate therapists' intentions and willingness to be of help. When a patient or the wife or husband calls to ask for information, the person answering the call is in a very important position. There should be a helpful, professional response, and the patient or the spouse given the opportunity to see someone as soon as possible. Above all, the temptation of giving off-the-cuff, "curbstone advice" should be avoided. So often the inexperienced therapist, after listening a few minutes to the patient or spouse, will give solemn advice that is less than useless because the person asking for help is left feeling that he "has tried all that and it didn't help."

The best initial contact with a prospective patient or family member is to listen, to take the presentation of problems seriously, and to decline to make impulsive judgment on what ought to be done. The initial objective in the first few contacts is to establish a trusting relationship, to bring the patient into therapy on a realistic basis, and help him or her to develop a well-planned program of rehabilitation, a program that will be ongoing and not sporadic, in which a gradually developing motivational insight can be fostered. This is often fraught with difficulty, and dealing with a patient in the early stages of therapy requires especially great skill. One reason for this difficulty is that the patient at this point is often quite dazed or confused about precisely what is happening to him. His problem drinking may have overtaken him almost imperceptibly. It is hardly surprising therefore that, at the beginning particularly, he again resorts to rationalizations and denial of the precise realities of his problem. Even when denial is no longer possible, he may be impelled to misinterpret his symptoms and problems, and to misconstrue his course of action. He may seek to control alcohol intake by enforcement of rigid self-discipline and may use help from others only for recovery from the pangs of a drinking episode. At such a point, an alcoholic or other problem drinker may find it quite impossible to define himself as such, and to accept the fact that his alcohol use is out of control, following a pathologically deviant pattern.

Even after he surrenders his alibis, the compulsion to adopt them can return again and again. The problem for the alcoholic is that he cannot accurately perceive that he is using alcohol as a means of holding life together—as a self-medication, as it were. These realizations may be marginally experienced, but not sufficiently clarified to be of value to him as motivational tools. Although he may indeed dimly realize to some degree that things are going wrong, he still finds that he cannot face the *need to stop drinking*. In his fright, he continues to cling to the rewards that he thinks he is getting. This is quite understandable, for his use of alcohol allows him to escape from his own sense of isolation and defeat; it may pull him together when he is in a state of panic by helping him to withdraw into his own world of fantasy where he can, for a brief time at least, be protected from the pain of living in a world that was not created solely for him. Then too, his environment may be so overwhelming and threatening that without some form of medication he cannot begin even to face it. As we have implied, it is most unfortunate, but of the essence of the alcoholic's trouble, that in his choice of alcohol he has hit upon a *defective* psychopharmacological agent, one that is quite inadequate pharmacologically and chemically as a medication for the serious needs for which an alcoholic has to use it. It gives him only temporary relief at best, while at the same time becoming a poisonous substance in his system. A patient who creatively grasps these facts and is ready to plan for a new way of life has a good chance of recovery.

The Vital Need to Motivate the Patient's Family

As his drinking problem becomes more sharply focused, an alcoholic finds himself pressed by his family, by his friends, and by the increasing urgency of his own problems, to abandon drinking; he is appalled, however, by the prospect of existence without the support of alcohol. He is, then, hardly helped by the fact that members of his family—already at their wit's end—propose what seems to them a reasonable solution namely, that he ought by his own will power to be able to abstain from something that is clearly destroying him. The alcoholic has tried will power and everything else that has occurred to him, so that he knows much better than his family knows how inadequate such attempts are. One of the important ways, therefore, in which we help strengthen the alcoholic's motivation is by helping to develop the quality of motivation of his family.

Families go through many phases of reaction in relation to an alcoholic member, and their motivations will vary from phase to phase. The first phase is one of *disbelief,* owing to the fact that the problem often arises so imperceptibly, although they may still recognize that something is wrong before the victim himself does. Often their first response is to try to carry on as usual and, just as the patient himself does, *to deny* the problem. Under these circumstances, they do not press for outside help. As the victim's condition worsens, disbelief is succeeded by a state of *shock* as well as by a *disorganization* of family functions and the breakdown of healthy interpersonal dynamics. The family's denial of the situation at this point may persist as a defense against panic in the family. They will attempt to restore functional integrity by various kinds of *reorganization* within the group. Thus, an older son or the nonalcoholic spouse will try to take over the major responsibilities of the problem drinker. Quite often, such families become impervious to outside help by building around the family a strong wall that cannot be penetrated. They are usually unaware that their isolation and refusal to seek help and their denial of the whole problem serves, only at best, to work out various minor problems. Everyone uses denial in this way for handling trivial problems. It is not, therefore, surprising that such a solution should be attempted in so serious a condition as problem drinking by the person himself or by the family. The critical feature of this denial process is not the walling-off of the family but *the underestimation by the family and the victim of the severity of the problem.*

When this course of action fails, and it does invariably, the family then mobilizes itself for a kind of *therapeutic* assault upon the difficulty. Having discovered that its own internal reorganization is unsuccessful, the family now undertakes to become the therapeutic agent. There is still no effort to bring in help from the outside; and, in fact, a family may even stand in the way of doing so. For example, when a husband has become alcoholic, the wife, the nonalcoholic spouse, may not even tell her mother about it. The minister may be shunned, and even the family doctor may not get a chance to discover the true state of affairs. Instead, members of the family will focus upon the alcoholic and make emotionally charged efforts to persuade him to arrest his drinking in the hope of abating his unacceptable behavior. This kind of family approach is so common that a wife will often immediately ask, when she finally does seek professional help, "How can I get my husband to stop his drinking?" Part of the frustration of the family members and part of their guilt feelings center around the fact that they feel that, in some way or other, they have failed to be effectively persuasive. In their effort to be therapeutic, a family often responds quite differently to problem drinking from the way they would to other types of illness, such as cancer, when an active attempt would be made to get early advice and help. One even finds that a woman will marry a man who is an incipient problem drinker or already a problem drinker in the hope that she can by her own special efforts bring about his recovery. This is a forlorn hope and when such efforts at informal family "therapy" fail, the failure too quickly leads to a rejection of the sick member. We see in bodily infections that there is a kind of "walling off" of the infective process by various means. For example, in appendicitis, the inflamed appendix is walled off by the so-called *great omentum* in the abdomen; this may serve to prevent the spread of infection and is a body response, though often inadequate, to the inflammatory processes.

In the case of problem drinkers, we have a situation similar to an infection; for problem drinking, including alcoholism, is a communicable illness in the sense that the troubles of the victim can be communicated to his family and to others. Thus, it is not unusual for the alcoholic to be segregated, rejected, and isolated from family participation. He is often overprotected in this process of segregation, rejection, and isolation. He may lose his status as head of the family and be reduced to that of a dependent child, a bad child at that. This rejection is a kind of *antitherapy*. It is associated in the family, as one would expect, with increasing irritability, hostility, depression, and confusion. If, for some reason, the patient gets to a treatment center or to an individual therapist at this time, the family's report on the patient will reflect the intensity of their anger against him. In such a situation, the family will try to compensate for the illness process by making an effort to function without the ill person. They will try leaving him to his own devices, but this is not generally successful. In fact, all these hopefully protective walling-off strategies are usually imperfect, with the alcoholic continuing to be a severe trial to his family who are not only hostile but despairing, desperate, and often quite guilty. Along about this time, there often follows a secondary disorganization in the family and the appearance of symptoms of illness and decompensation in the nonalcoholic members. The wife will ascribe all or most of her troubles and those of the children to the alcoholic behavior of her husband. Members of such families sometimes seek help for themselves at this point and only then gain insight as to what the problems of the alcoholic husband or father are. Even so, at this point, if family members seek help, they may do so primarily for the patient's sake. Their own need for outside guidance may now be very strong, and the situation becomes a wholesome one insofar as it opens up the family to competent professional attention. It may be only later that they begin to be aware of their *own* need for help.

Throughout these various stages of family response, the alcoholic member himself, perhaps as well as anyone else, sees what is happening as far as harm to himself and others is concerned, but he will find the suggestions that his family makes empty, unhelpful, or excessively critical, depending on the phase of their reaction. He may then react to his family with feelings of hurt, guilt, or anger. Or he may *accept* the idea that his drinking is a weakness or bad habit to be controlled through disciplined exercise of the will. He may try hard only to fail, and he may even try repeatedly. Such efforts of *will* characteristically fail. In their therapy, what the family often succeeds in doing is to support the alcoholic in his dependency on drink and to protect him against outside stresses; this may go on for many, many years. It is quite extraordinary how wives and husbands of alcoholics will stick with their spouses; how they will phone the boss and cover up for the victim. More extraordinary is how relatives of alcoholics will make good their bad checks and support them in all kinds of unhealthy ways. Sometimes when it is really essential "to pull the rug" from under the patient, the family finds itself unwilling to take part in doing so. This is not to say that physicians themselves and other helping agents do not cover for alcoholics. Thiebout used to say to me that it was a temptation of a physician to "carry an alcoholic upright to his grave." This is an important insight, for there is no doubt that alcoholics, despite their unpleasant behavior, are usually quite winsome and successful in "conning" their families, their friends, and their professional advisers.

Hitting Bottom

For the alcoholic who eventually recovers and establishes a truly sober way of life that permits reasonable functioning, something quite remarkable happens from which he later dates his recovery. This is the experience of "hitting bottom," that we mentioned before, an expression which is now accepted as a well-defined technical term. The circumstances of this experience vary from patient to patient, but for all who experience it, it is the serious crisis which brought them up short and revealed to them that their future as drinking alcoholics would hold nothing for them but despair and hopelessness. Thiebout (10) well described the recognition by the patient that his life has failed and that he can look forward to nothing but pain and misery as long as he continues to use alcohol. At this point the patient may cry out for help. The need to hit bottom as a prelude to recovery now finds rather wide acceptance although, as Thiebout himself noted, this concept found little sanction psychiatrically in the early 1930s. Prior to the recognition of this phenomenon and its acceptance, the function of the psychiatrist was often conceived as that of giving support even though the support did, so to speak, carry the patient upright to his grave. The alcoholic who hits bottom admits his own powerlessness and decides to turn his life and his will over to a power outside and greater than himself. This concept has demonstrated its essential usefulness within the fellowship of Alcoholics Anonymous and in the practice of other therapists.

The experience can be formulated something like this: The patient sees with considerable clarity the actual condition of his life and he surrenders. As we have said, Thiebout likened this surrender to a *conversion experience*—that is to say, the alcoholic pulls himself up short from a runaway course and turns around in a new direction. In the act of surrender, according to Thiebout, the "big ego" of the patient is reduced, and by "big ego" he means the original ego of the infant, the narcissistic remnant which is a carry-over from the infantile state and which Freud called the unmodified portion of the original psyche. According to Thiebout, the salvation of the patient lies in his keeping that ego reduced and humble. *Humility,* then, is a state which is necessary for the patient if he is to maintain his therapy and continue his recovery. The surrender, as Thiebout admits, may not be permanent; and the motivation arising from the experience of crisis can unfortunately be erased as the patient senses his early improvement. Often we have observed that when the patient begins to overcome his depression and his remorse as hospitalization proceeds and as his outpatient therapy continues, he becomes vulnerable to drinking again. In Thiebout's terms, what happens to the patient is that there has been a "false cure" and the infantile ego is again asserting itself. This is why the motivational question is much more profound than we might at first think it to be.

There is a commendable tendency currently among both therapists and the public to forestall hitting low bottom because it *is* so low a level, and to try, instead, to help the patient before he falls to this level. Perhaps what they really mean is that we should devise ways to help the patient to see his powerlessness long before his situation has deteriorated to the low level of hitting bottom. Now there is no question but that a sensitive investigation of patients who recover does reveal the importance of this hitting bottom, this surrender-and-conversion pattern. As long as family members and others support the patient in his addiction and cover for him in various ways, it is unlikely that he will achieve a motivational formulation that will lead him into effective therapy.

The experience of hitting bottom is undoubtedly a devastating one for the alcoholic and may at first completely paralyze his effort to obtain help. He may even become more deeply and irreversibly depressed or commit suicide. A patient who has hit bottom needs encouragement and help. More study is unquestionably needed of the techniques whereby motivation can be handled and strengthened before a person becomes so ill that his prognosis is hopeless. Therefore, professional caretakers do, in my judgment, have a responsibility to enter therapeutically into the patient's pathological process as early as possible and not to wait for a patient to reach a "low bottom." This requires skill and flexibility as well as patience, and the intervention of the therapist is always to be associated with an objective presentation to the patient, or the prospective patient and his family, of the exact realities of the situation as far as these can be assessed. Sometimes it is helpful to let the patient and the family know and understand that their denial mechanisms and efforts at self-therapy are attempts to cure and, therefore, not blameworthy; but it must also be clearly pointed out at the same time that these efforts are inadequate in the face of a serious, progressive disorder that moves when untreated to a fatal conclusion in most cases. It is also true that a small proportion of alcoholics apparently "recover" in a sense that they arrest their drinking without formal therapy, but this is unusual and cannot be relied upon. Also, it is said that a very small number of alcoholics do seem, with or without therapy, to achieve temporarily at least some form of controlled drinking. The clinical evidence for this, however, is so uncertain and is based upon such a small number of cases, inadequately followed up, that it should not be held out to the alcoholic or his family as a reasonable goal. In the present state of our knowledge this so-called "cure" of alcoholism should be regarded as a research problem and not a practical goal of therapy.

We do not yet know enough exactly how physicians and other helping personnel can assist patients and their families to effective motivation for restoration of health. As I write this, I have just come from interviewing a prospective patient and his wife. The patient is fairly typical of many whom we see. He has had nothing to drink today, but had about a pint of whiskey yesterday. This family has two children, the older twenty-four, the younger seventeen. He works in a factory. His problem has been manifest for four or five years although he has been drinking most of his life. He has never been hospitalized for his drinking problem, but his family doctor has given him vitamins from time to time. He denies having ever had convulsions, blackouts or delirium tremens, but he does suffer from withdrawal tremors. His pattern of drinking is to consume large amounts of alcohol on weekends and on vacations. His wife, for several years, has considered divorcing him, but now wishes to stand by him. He came for his admission interviews today because his doctor referred him and because his wife took the initiative to encourage him to come. At present, it appears that his job is not in jeopardy.

This man's wife and the physician both think that he is an addicted alcoholic. He says he is not sure. When I interviewed him, he was not drunk but had been drinking, and is here chiefly, as far as he is concerned, because he feels so acutely sick. He says that he has not ever felt this sick before. Although his chief goal at the present time is to receive help in handling the results of the recent drinking, he is willing to promise to stay in the hospital as long as it is required and to attend my own outpatient clinic regularly (about once a week or every other week) for at least a year. Thus he seems tractable, and willing, and he does not show resistance to this program. We therefore admitted him, and we shall see within the next few days how well his motivation develops.

I think that after he gets into the hospital and talks with other patients and takes part in group sessions, he will begin to understand the illness of alcoholism which he now understands only imperfectly. I believe that talking around the coffee table with other patients will be of help to him; he will begin to find himself at home in group therapy in the hospital, and he will probably join A.A. as well, for there will be opportunities while he is in the hospital to attend A.A. meetings and to go out into the community to attend others. I imagine that physical findings will be relatively minor and that he is in reasonably good physical health at this time. I suspect that the psychometric tests will indicate that he has an average intelligence and that there is little brain damage, but that he is probably not functioning at full efficiency. The patient has experienced for many years marital discord with his wife, who is by now a rather cold, unaffectionate woman. This is all we can tell about him at this time, having met him for the first time just one hour ago.

The question of his motivation is one which we have handled the best way we know how. We have admitted him. We have introduced him to the members of the staff who will work with him. His contact with me will be maintained throughout his stay in the hospital and I will see him several times a week, both in the group therapy in the hospital and also in staff meetings. The point is that he will not ever fall out of contact with me while in the hospital and the other relations established in the first interview will be maintained in the outpatient clinic. At present it does not seem that he needs job counseling but it appears that his alcoholism is primary and that therapy will be supportive and will be directed toward helping him further to understand his addictive problem.

We have also made ourselves aware of his motivation. We have set up for him a program which he knows about and to which he has agreed. We do not yet know how the physicians and other helping personnel will be able to assist him in achieving effective motivation. However, we think that they can be of help by their frankness, by their honesty with the patient and his family, and by refusing to condemn or to permit the patient to manipulate them and so prolong the pathological situation.

In the admission interview just concluded, we have been very frank about his situation, both with him and his wife, who have been seen together and separately. We do not believe that we have unduly pressured the patient. We have, however, so far as I can tell, helped him to begin to see his problems in the light of practical reality. He certainly believes that drinking is making him ill in many ways. It may be that when he came to the hospital for his interview, his main goal was to try to get over his acute sickness. Some people believe that an alcoholic is most available to therapy when he is in a withdrawal state as is the present patient. This may or may not be true. Other things being equal, the threat of loss of a valued job with tenure probably renders a patient most available to rehabilitative therapy. I sometimes doubt whether the withdrawal state *per se* is the optimum time. Nevertheless, it is a time when the patient is available to certain kinds of effective motivational pressure. In any case, he is motivated to get over his tremor, his nausea, his headaches, and so forth. In the case of the present patient, however, we have been at pains to minimize for him the present difficulties by medication and to maximize the importance of the ongoing issues which he is going to face for the rest of his life. Though the patient is now in a state of withdrawal from alcohol and is somewhat tremulous and anxious about his physical condition, we have not concentrated solely on this but upon the long term goal. I think that we have taken the right steps in this case and that we will be able to judge how well we have done after the patient has spent a few weeks in the hospital and again later, after he has been in therapy in our outpatient clinic for several months. In this outpatient therapy, he will continue to be supported by several of the staff he will meet in the hospital, including myself.

There may be, unfortunately, as we have implied previously, many false starts toward recovery. When we chart or graph the recovery process, we find in most cases that it is not really a smooth ascending curve tapering off at the top, but a sawtooth curve with ups and downs, with, one hopes, the ups becoming progressively higher and the periods of sobriety longer, and the periods of competent behavior more stable. A patient, then, who hits bottom, surrenders, and experiences a conversion, joins the battle of therapy only at the point when he recognizes not only his need for sobriety but also the often tremendous and continued effort that he must put into his rehabilitation. The successful patient, as far as rehabilitation and sobriety are concerned, is one in whom the forces directing him continually to seek help, win out.

Planning Therapy

The therapy of alcoholics to be successful must be planned and continuing. Nothing is more important than that the patient together with his therapists make such a plan. This plan must be agreed upon and clear-cut, but also flexible enough to meet needs that arise. For example, let us say a patient has been sober for many months, he is working, his wife restores to him his family responsibilities. The children may feel happy about his assuming family leadership again (although there may have been some concern about this, especially if some other member of the family has held the position of acting authority for many years). The difficulty that may now arise at this point is that, true to the sawtooth character of the recovery curve, the patient may go through a drinking crisis and even seem to be regressing to his former helpless and hopeless state.

It is not easy to tell a patient starting treatment that this may or will happen. Sometimes it is too discouraging for the patient. Nevertheless, if this does happen, account must be taken of it in the rearrangement of plans, and it must not be allowed to become an occasion for despair and chaos in the family. This is what I mean by planning for therapy and being flexible enough to take care of events as they happen. Moreover, the talent of the family in forestalling such drinking situations can be greatly enhanced when the family along with the patient begin to recognize symptoms of nervousness, irritability, depression, panic, or other behavioral manifestations and so foretell a drinking bout or a breakdown of the patient's capacity to function effectively in other ways.

We know that people with chronic heart disease can suffer acute or semiacute decompensation. So it often is with the alcoholic. If our attitude toward the heart patient were punitive, we would give up on him because every six months or so he has an acute cardiac crisis that keeps him out of work for a week or more. However, we stand by the heart patient and help him. So we should do with the alcoholic patient who may have a similar crisis.

The difficulty with episodic and intermittent treatment based only upon carrying the patient through drinking sprees is that it cannot but fail, and not only does it fail but it also is in itself distherapeutic for the whole family. Unfortunately, in many cases, alcoholics have been treated and are still being treated in exactly this fashion. They come to the attention of professional people only when they have a drinking crisis. When they are sobered up again, no attempt is made to continue treatment or to work on a plan of ongoing therapy. We need to remember constantly that alcoholism and other forms of problem drinking are *chronic* progressive conditions, potentially fatal, and that without planned, resourceful, *ongoing* therapy there is really no hope for the victims or their families. So far as the motivation of the physicians and other therapists is concerned, alcoholic patients are often unwanted in hospitals and in doctors' offices, partly because the emphasis in treatment has too often been solely or primarily upon symptomatic relief of crisis problems. We grant that crises should be handled and that this is, indeed, absolutely necessary. But the drinking crisis is not the only one that we should work on. Sometimes I readmit a patient who is troubled or depressed with the hope that a drinking crisis may be forestalled.

In the case of alcoholics it is completely unhelpful simply to devote oneself to relief of drinking crises because thus the emphasis is incorrectly placed. It is as if the illness of the alcoholic is primarily or solely dissonant drinking. We would do much better to remember that he is often just as sick when he is sober as when he is drunk. True, drunkenness and drunken behavior are symptomatic of the illness of alcoholism just as continued, sustained sobriety is indicative of progressive recovery. However, there are other evidences of recovery than sobriety alone. These are to be found in improved family relations, better job efficiency, and so forth. Alcoholics cannot be left to their own devices and they should not be allowed or forced, as they often are now, to make dramatic statements and exaggerated promises that they will never drink again. I am troubled when a patient leaving the ward says to me, "Doc, you will never see me again here." As long as help for the alcoholic is limited to periodic management of his acute drinking attacks, whether in the hospital or in an office or through home visits, with no ongoing rehabilitative outpatient program, including, if necessary, some form of residential "halfway" care, it is most unlikely that progress will be made.

Summary

In connection with the motivation both of the patient and of his family, we need to remember, first, that an alcoholic is a sick person. He is an overwhelmed person, overwhelmed by a complex disorder; and he is usually living in a family situation that has also become disordered, partly as a result of his illness, partly because of preexisting pathological processes in the family. Also, by the time an alcoholic reaches some therapeutic confrontation, other members of the family—say, the spouse—may be more ill than the alcoholic himself, either because of, or from causes prior to, the patient's alcoholism.

It can hardly be doubted that as therapy proceeds, the patient's progress and recovery may also create new situations which will be disturbing within the family because of the necessary readjustments in family interpersonal relationships. We have spoken of this before, but we may take occasion to give another example. Thus an alcoholic under therapy may no longer be an acceptable partner to a spouse with a developed or prior need to dominate or control. Sometimes a spouse will live and put up for years with a sick, drinking alcoholic. Either because of his or her earlier personality needs or needs that develop during the alcoholic's illness, he or she will tolerate the situation, indeed come to require the situation although he or she may be totally unconscious of this need. Many women particularly find it impossible to live with sober alcoholics, and it cannot have escaped the notice of some readers that many spouses whose alcoholic partner either dies or is separated by divorce will form marriages or other liaisons with other persons with similar alcoholic illness. One should not thereby conclude that all spouses of alcoholics have a need for the kind of person that becomes or is an alcoholic. Nevertheless, the truth is that a spouse does sometimes choose as a second or third husband or wife such persons.

I remember a patient of mine, a man who had a wife (a nurse) and two adopted children. The patient did very well in therapy and was entirely abstinent for at least six months. At about that time he came to see me for his regular appointment and said that his wife was out in the waiting room to see me. I asked her to come in after having seen the patient. I saw her alone in my office and she was so angry and upset that she could hardly speak. She finally came out with the extraordinary remark: "I wish he would drink, I feel like throwing that Anta-buse down the sink." Little by little, amidst tears, she told her story. Her husband no longer needed her. He went off to A.A. two or three times a week. She never saw him. In the old days when he was drinking, at least he was grateful to her for nursing him and caring for him. She was, as I say, a registered nurse but had not practiced her profession in a hospital for a number of years. Now she felt lost and unhappy. She was suspicious about his going out with other women. She was completely unable to tolerate a husband who was behaving more and more like a competent man and less and less like a helpless child. Fortunately, both of these people were able to grow in insight as to what was happening. One of our social workers began to work with the wife while I continued to work with the husband, the primary patient. I am happy that both husband and wife developed new creative insights as to what marriage could be and what the relationship between them could and should become. It has been some ten years since this crisis occurred. From time to time I have a visit from the couple and they are doing well.

It is true, however, that an alcoholic under therapy may no longer be an acceptable partner, either temporarily or for a long period of time, and that this unacceptability may not be easily cleared up. An alcoholic who is "dry" (but not really sober) may be querulous, demanding, miserly, irascible, and undependable. Or sometimes a spouse or children may have so adapted to the drinking alcoholic's behavior that it is difficult, even impossible, for them to accept the alcoholic as a maturing, sober person. The recovery process of an alcoholic is often as perplexing a time for the patient's family as the period of his drinking was. It can and ought to make possible, however, the opening of new options. Motivation, for both family and alcoholic himself includes helping them all to understand some of these things that will happen or may happen, helping them to see ways in which they can be dealt with intelligently and effectively.

So often one is inclined to think of the problem of treating alcoholics as mainly developing a strategy for bringing about sobriety. As we see from this chapter, this may only be the beginning, and usually is. A person who is a sober alcoholic has a great deal to learn about living and a lot of insight and understanding to catch up on. Thus it is important that family members be helped to understand as clearly as possible the nature of the alcoholic's illness and the characteristics of the recovery process, and what will be their own problems arising out of his drinking phase as well as his recovery phase, so that there may be fostered within the family an environment that is truly therapeutic for all.

As an alcoholic becomes sober and starts to travel that long road toward rehabilitation, many realignments of family relationships and functions have to occur. One must make room for the alcoholic member to take his place again within these relationships, and tolerance on all sides is required. It is hard to say who should be *most* tolerant; all must be. Many alcoholics become irritated with their family as they stop drinking. Many alcoholics become parsimonious about money and scrupulous about the behavior of their children, and so forth. It is often because, for the first time in years, they have really paid attention to what is going on. Their criticism may be biting and their unkindness to the nonalcoholic spouse may hurt.

On the other side of the family there is the problem of uncertainty about the alcoholic's sobriety and his capacity to sustain a cooperative role. Occasional sprees and slips often necessitate quick family readjustments to allow for the patient's changing status. This uncertainty of the patient's capacities from week to week or from month to month is in itself confusing. It is particularly important that through all this the family establish its own resources of strength and stability and, at the same time, offer as far as possible a setting that is conducive to recovery for everyone. Perhaps most important of all, members of the family should be helped to relinquish their self-imposed responsibilities as therapists.

The restoration of an alcoholic, then, is not simply a matter of establishing a nondrinking pattern for him, although this is absolutely essential. It includes far more. It includes the restoration of a family whose members and whose group health has been bruised and damaged, often over many years. Restoration of such a family is like an awaking from a kind of nightmare.

PART III

Care and Rehabilitation

8
The Treatment of Problem Drinking

Interest in and concern for the treatment of problem drinking has varied considerably over the decades. A less than hopeful attitude toward treatment was expressed in the Cooperative Commission Report (4), which stated that although treatment for problem drinkers is indeed essential, it is not in itself prevention. The most discouraging comment was that treatment efforts probably cannot cope with new cases as they arise and cannot reduce the prevalence of problem drinking. Adequate treatment for all problem drinkers would require the efforts of more than all the professionally trained physicians, psychiatrists, social workers, nurses, and psychologists in the country. There is little likelihood, in the Commission's view, that the number of workers in these areas could ever be sufficiently increased to treat even a considerable minority of such drinkers (according to estimates available at the time of the publication of the report) with weekly contact with a psychiatrist and once-a-month contact with a social worker.

In the past twenty years or so, however, it is becoming more and more clear that with the application of new knowledge of treatment of alcoholics and mobilization of new and more understanding staff, the condition is becoming more and more successfully treatable. It is one of the remarkable advances of our times that more and more trained alcoholism counselors and therapists are joining our ranks, and these young men and women are infusing much needed enthusiasm into the therapeutic endeavor. We also have the capacity of more effective deployment of staff and of bringing in other care-giving agencies and I believe that this will continue to alleviate treatment staff shortage problems.

Recovery rates in our Unit are continuing to increase and it is our opinion that a major factor in growing success rates is not only the availability of a vigorous and vivid inpatient experience but also prolonged outpatient programs in which each patient sees a counselor and a physician at least once a week at first and then perhaps once every other week for the duration of at least a year.

Also the increasing acceptance of problem drinkers as worthy patients in general hospitals as well as special clinical centers will, I believe, greatly help. I have spoken warmly of the value of aftercare facilities staffed by those who are deeply concerned for their patients and who see them frequently for considerable periods of time. In addition, research and investigation into the causes, dynamics and treatment of alcoholism and other problem drinking are not being neglected. I am thinking particularly of clinical research—for example, the knowledge we in our own Unit are gathering about the best ways of treating teenage alcoholics and those in their early twenties. These young sufferers require a special approach to which they respond in a wholesome, positive way. The fact that our Unit is completely racially integrated affords many contributing advantages to the total therapeutic thrust. This will be referred to later in our section on Outpatient Clinic Groups (p. 155). But here it should be said that it is wise to give a patient help in some tangentially related condition to which he may be chronically vulnerable. Large numbers of black patients, for example, are victims of high blood pressure associated probably with special stresses under which they have to live. In our inpatient as well as our outpatient therapy, we try to restore such patients to normo-tensive status as soon as possible. Similarly one might speak of the tendencies for these and other patients to be particularly vulnerable to seizures of one sort or another. Such patients are worked up diagnostically for this special purpose and treated successfully for the most part. The advantage of this approach to treatment is that when patients feel better in other ways in addition to their improvement from not drinking, this improvement radiates out into all aspects of their physical and emotional life.

We still encounter the lingering attitude previously alluded to that alcoholics are to blame for their condition. The implication sometimes is that the patients do not deserve treatment or at least do not deserve sophisticated, well thought out therapy. We have strongly condemned this attitude as archaic and dangerous to the health of our society.

Enlightened thinking and action in Public Health in the past two hundred years or more have increasingly stressed the value of prevention of human illness and in considering how to eradicate problem drinking obvious strategies of prevention have increasingly moved to the fore. Early and well planned therapy is a factor. This is greatly to be commended. But better, it has been urged, to build a fence around the dangerous curve at the top than to keep an ambulance at the bottom of the precipice. Our success in the future will assuredly lie in our wisdom in approaching the many challenging issues of problem drinking and establishing effective coordination among all of the related caregiving services in our communities. We still need to deploy the services more efficiently and use them both for comprehensive treatment and rehabilitation as well as vigorous action toward prevention by early diagnosis and other means. We confront in alcoholism the major addictive disorder in our country which deserves rehabilitative as well as preventive efforts. To prevent and to treat alcoholism, we require a constantly growing body of research, particularly clinical research as well as public education at all levels. Along with this, the help of efficient government bodies is essential.

What we obviously must do is not to neglect either prevention or therapy. We can learn much from therapy to apply to prevention, and our preventive goals will, and indeed should, lead us to a greater sophistication in our therapeutic techniques. Although there may not be enough professional people available today to care for the problem drinkers who need help, this very insufficiency should motivate us both to find new helpers and to reassess *the enlistment of paraprofessional helpers and counselors, and programs of self-care* as exemplified so well in Alcoholics Anonymous. Obviously, treatment will also be greatly facilitated by having many professional specialists in alcohol problems assigned to community agencies to help these agencies and their staff to become fully involved and maximally effective in bringing the problems of drinking fully into the areas of community mental health, welfare, human relations, penology, and so forth.

Some Obstacles to Adequate Care

We have already spoken about the discrimination against problem drinkers that still exists among otherwise sincere and public-spirited people. It is almost a truism to say that problem drinkers do not in general evoke sympathy. Their frequent or persistent drunkenness calls forth just the opposite reaction in many situations. One hears and sees, however, less of this moralistic approach, as a more humane and enlightened conception of public responsibility toward problem drinking develops. Since problem drinkers in early stages remind us of ourselves, many people are willing to encourage and support attention to early problem drinking. It is also remarkable how much concern has been expressed in recent years for the deteriorated, homeless men who fill our police courts on a "revolving door" basis. There are even those who say that we should concentrate primarily upon these people in our endeavors to treat and to prevent problem drinking. There remains, then, a great and urgent need to build broad preventive programs that will be efficacious.

Despite these promising trends, we must agree with the Cooperative Commission Report when it points out that public attitudes and feelings about drinking and alcohol misuse have negatively influenced the way services for problem drinkers have developed. While many people believe that problem drinkers can be effectively helped, a large proportion of the general public and, even more unhappily, a large number of professional people do not believe so. This "therapeutic nihilism" is unfortunate and stems in part from the view that problem drinking is self-inflicted, especially at the beginning. I suspect, however, that most agencies that still are unwilling to work with problem drinkers are unwilling because, for one reason or another, they do not believe they can achieve results with these patients. However, I would say that the tendency in the last few years, and particularly since the appearance of the Cooperative Commission Report, is to show much more willingness to help problem drinkers and to overcome reluctance in providing care and treatment. I also find among young medical students, residents, nurses, and social workers a real desire to work with such patients and a readiness to accept them as they would any other ill and disturbed person. Then, too, hospitalization insurance coverage appears to be less and less restrictively applied to alcoholic patients, as does admission to general hospitals. This is true also of vocational rehabilitation services and voluntary admission to mental hospitals, as well as participation in mental hospital aftercare programs. State and federal funding of alcoholism therapy has also greatly increased.

It remains true, however, that the care and treatment provided for problem drinkers are still often narrow and segmented. What we must stress today is that these patients need to be approached as entire persons in the setting of their families, their communities, and their jobs. Alcoholics and their families need and deserve therapy that is interdisciplinary and comprehensive. Care should not be limited to "sobering up" or simply to limited aspects of the patient's difficulties. Care should not be sporadic or brief, but continuous and ongoing. These patients deserve the best kind of medical and other health care including inpatient care, outpatient services, and sociologically oriented help, as well as the best we can offer in psychotherapy of all kinds as may be required. While it is true that we may prefer to work with those whom we consider most motivated and best educated and socially, physiologically, and psychologically intact, we are now happily learning that there are great and unexpected rewards in working with those who appear at first to lack these characteristics. In saying that alcoholism services wherever found have been often isolated from other community helping agencies, the Commission is quite right. This brings out the important point which we have stressed before—namely, that the interrelatedness of these problems should always be kept foremost.

I do not think that it is appropriate to blame our health and care-giving services unduly for their efforts, because the problems associated with treating problem drinkers are difficult to handle by old, traditional approaches. A general hospital decides, for example, to admit alcoholics. However, it then finds itself trying to give these patients the identical kind of acute care that it would, say, a patient with acute appendicitis. I have often been impressed by the fact that when a general hospital admits an alcoholic, there is still a tendency to sequester and isolate him; and the patient himself often assents readily to this program. This is especially true of the cases of persons of consequence and means who seem to have been brought into the hospital simply to be hidden for a period of time. New techniques of group therapy in the setting of a broadly therapeutic community need to be more widely used. For hospital care to help these patients, it must include the care of an interdisciplinary team, the assistance of social workers, pastoral counselors, psychiatrists, general practitioners, and other counselors. These patients while in the hospital need to be with one another. They need to discuss their problems together. They need to be brought in contact with A.A. and other agencies. They need the assistance of practical rehabilitation counselors. In short, the correct therapy for an alcoholic in a hospital, whether it be general or special, must involve group relationships, particularly the opportunity for the patient to face his problems in a *therapeutic community*. In addition to appropriate therapy while in the hospital, then, the patient must also receive transitional care as needed, such as partial hospitalization, halfway houses, and outpatient clinics provided by either alcoholism centers or community mental-health-clinic services. Fortunately, many general hospitals throughout the country are aware of this need now and are developing hospital communities in which alcoholics can live and work together in a setting that provides first-class medical, psychiatric, and psychological care as well as diagnosis.

Emergency and Other Services for Alcoholics

It is appropriate to review the emergency services offered by general hospitals, special detoxification units, mental hospitals, and jails. A few general observations on these services are in order here. One problem sometimes encountered in emergency services of a general hospital is that intoxicated patients may be thrown into the melee of a general waiting room before receiving care, since accident victims, victims of stroke, etc., may be given priority. The emergency service may be overloaded, and intoxicated patients may come at a time of day when they constitute a special stress on the capacity of the staff to give them personalized attention. It is sometimes difficult for the emergency staff to transfer such patients to a department of the hospital where they will receive ongoing care. However, any arrangement that can provide this is good. To an acutely ill alcoholic, it is comforting and helpful to have some one therapist accompany and encourage him in the otherwise possibly frightening experience of the emergency service. Special detoxification units are beginning to be developed in various parts of the country, specializing in intensive care for very intoxicated persons—for example, those in a coma.

The major sources of outpatient help for problem drinkers are alcoholism programs and general psychiatric clinics. The organization of outpatient clinics varies widely from place to place, and the techniques similarly are variable. Some operate on a full-time basis, others on part-time; but most of them are oriented psychologically in their treatment methods and draw for their staff upon members of the mental health and medical professions. A wide variety of programs of group therapy both for patients and for families has become more common, and individual counseling of various kinds is also offered. One of the major shortcomings of many alcoholism clinics still is their relative isolation from other community agencies. Where this is so, it is obviously of importance to integrate such clinics with the general community.

It ought to be said that the outpatient clinic under whatever auspices is a most potent system in the total therapeutic program. Some patients can be treated in an outpatient service without going through some inpatient-care program. Many patients have done quite well by attending outpatient clinics alone and coordinating this with Alcoholics Anonymous and residence in a halfway house. There may be a particular value of an outpatient clinic in those cases of problem drinkers who have not reached advanced addictive phases of alcoholism. The outpatient clinic that would seek to uncover and draw into its field of concern such problem drinkers has an exciting and remarkable opportunity not only in treatment but also prevention. My own thought about this is that outpatient clinics can also serve as community centers for families as well as for patients. To make such a clinic attractive and efficient and to provide a warm friendly setting where people can talk together is of great importance.

In gratefully acknowledging the tremendous help that has been received by alcoholics and their families from Alcoholics Anonymous. Al-Anon and Alateens, one should never forget the dedicated and often anonymous help given by physicians in private practice. Family physicians have been the workhorses in helping problem drinkers long before the present surge of interest in therapy for problem drinkers. They have worked without the advantages of a team around them or of adequate hospital resources; but despite these handicaps, they have done a remarkably good job.

9
A Working Model

We shall now describe some principles of therapy as they are applied to the program and activities of the Bureau of Alcohol Studies and Rehabilitation of the Virginia State Department of Health, particularly the Bureau's Unit at the Medical College of Virginia, Virginia Commonwealth University. I have chosen this program of care and rehabilitation as a working model not only because of my familiarity with it but also because of its comprehensiveness.

The Virginia General Assembly Act of 1948 and Subsequent Developments

In 1948 the General Assembly of the Commonwealth of Virginia, enacted legislation providing for the study of the problems of alcoholism, the treatment of persons addicted to excessive use of alcohol, and the establishment of a Bureau of Alcohol Studies and Rehabilitation within the Virginia State Department of Health, in coordination with the medical schools of the state (11). According to this legislation, any person who through excessive use of alcoholic beverages had become unable to care for himself, his family, or his property, or had become a burden on the public, might voluntarily request admission to hospital and clinic facilities established under the Act. Persons admitted for treatment in these facilities were to be selected on the basis of individual benefit and/or for research objectives of the Bureau. This was a remarkable piece of legislation for its time and set a precedent for similar legislation in other states.

One of the striking aspects of the Act was that for the first time it offered Virginia residents the opportunity to apply for voluntary treatment relatively early in the course of their illness. Patients admitted for treatment to the hospitals and clinics were to pay for their care and treatment insofar as they were able, provided that no person be charged at a rate greater than the actual cost. Both the voluntary feature incorporated into the Act and carried out from 1948 to the present and individual responsibility for payment have turned out well. It is true that some alcoholics could not really sustain a voluntary program. However, as we have begun to see, more and more the voluntary character was sufficiently protected and the motivational factors sufficiently worked out that many persons, who otherwise would have had to be committed legally to treatment, began to present themselves for voluntary care. No patient is compelled by law to enter therapy. Some might think that this means that really desperately ill alcoholics are not able to obtain therapy in this program. This is not really the case, although it does mean that there may be a few who will never be able to enter the program. A certain geographical stability is required, but this is also true of patients who are committed to various state hospitals throughout the country.

At first, very few people, in proportion to the total number who applied and were admitted, paid for their care. The Bureau took the view that there should be no scaling up or down of payment according to ability to pay, but that, instead, those who could not pay were to be allowed and encouraged to work out a program of deferred installment payment. At present some 70 to 80 percent of the cost of their treatment is paid by the patients either directly or through insurance policies. Many of the patients pay their bill over a period of one to five years or more. At least for the first two admissions to the hospital, no patient is required to pay in advance, and the ability to pay upon admission is not a criterion for acceptance. At regular intervals, the cost of treatment is assessed by the Medical College of Virginia, and the State Health Department regularly pays to the medical school the established per diem cost. The Bureau then bills the patients directly.

The provision that payment be made has therapeutic value, for it assumes that patients will not remain indigent, and that through treatment they will gain and continue in employment. For the past several years, we have devoted much attention to vocational rehabilitation counseling. As patients become self-sustaining through job retraining, the expectation is that given time and continuing therapy most patients will meet their financial responsibility. Since patients make it a matter of pride to become self-sustaining, the payment of their bills to the Bureau becomes a focal point. Thus, the patient-payment requirement aids the program financially and the patient therapeutically. Instead of scaling down costs, the amount is met by extending the term of payment. The rate of payment is decided by the patient himself in the course of financial interviews with a professional accounts officer.

Since 1948 to the present, 15,700 patients have been accepted, all on a voluntary basis, at the Bureau's Unit at the Medical College of Virginia. In 1969 (as will be described in Chapter 10) this Unit was expanded as a research center to study causes, treatment, and prevention of alcoholism; and to train doctors, nurses, and social workers, as well as counselors. Presently the Unit comprises a 40-bed inpatient program as well as weekly sessions at at an outpatient clinic which has had approximately 1,500 visits in the past year. These outpatient sessions are supplemented by individual appointments made available by the staff of the Unit. This year a second outpatient clinic has been set up with approximately the same patient load.

In July 1971, the Bureau of Alcohol Studies and Rehabilitation was reorganized and modernized under the directorship of Dr. Thomas Dundon (15) to expand and facilitate its prevention, treatment and other functions. Fifteen Divisions of Alcoholism Services have been established—each with multimodality, multidisciplinary and coordinated centers. All of them are related to the Unit at the Medical College of Virginia in referral of patients, training of staff, and other activities.

At our Unit and others of the Bureau's treatment centers, we care for alcoholics and other problem drinkers with all kinds of personality, medical, and other problems. Some are not far removed from so-called "skid-row" alcoholics; others have serious psychiatric problems. In still other cases, the problems are primarily alcoholic and only secondarily emotional. Nevertheless, almost all these patients have been in trouble for many years and have made many previous voluntary attempts at treatment or have been forced into treatment involuntarily. A large number of the patients we accept are "dropouts" from Alcoholics Anonymous. A large proportion of the patients who come to us consider the Bureau as the last resort. Thus, many of the people we work with have "hit bottom" and are truly desperate. Any person who believes he or a relative may have an alcohol problem is welcome to come and discuss the matter with a clinic physician or other admitting officer.

The Intake Process

Prospective patients come from several sources, as follows:

Self-referred	7.2%
Relatives	9.1%
Friends	9.4%
Courts	4.7%
Social Agencies	3.9%
Physicians	34.6%
Spouses	6.7%
Clergy	3.6%
Alcoholics Anonymous	8.2%
Former Bureau Patients	4.7%
Others	7.9%

It is interesting that a high proportion come directly from private physicians (34.6%).

Persons either telephone, write to us, or come to the Treatment Center of the State Bureau, where the patient and/or his family are first seen. Generally we like to relate to the patient in a noncondemnatory, supportive way as he or she and the family discuss their problems openly. A considerable proportion of the patients come from Alcoholics Anonymous and tend to do well. In fact, among the referral sources those who do best come from social agencies, physicians, clergy, and Alcoholics Anonymous, as opposed to those who are referred by their spouses directly. When a physician, social agency, court, clergyman, or Alcoholics Anonymous makes a referral, primary contact with members of the family has probably already been made. Professional referrals carry a better prognosis because they seem to understand how to match a prospective patient with the resources of our program. Also such a referral usually sets in motion a variety of community resources. Fortunately, we have good relations with professional persons throughout the state with whom we make a point of keeping in regular contact. For example, we regularly send summary reports on hospital treatment and further recommendations to the referring physician. Patients usually work closely with Alcoholics Anonymous in addition to attending an outpatient clinic.

It is family problems which compound the difficulties experienced by patients who have been referred by their spouses. Even so, spouse referrals can be met with good prognosis, particularly if the spouse himself or herself is brought into an early treatment situation. He or she is helped to understand his or her own problems as well as those of the primary patient, and to become as involved as possible in the ongoing therapy along with receiving help from Alcoholics Anonymous and Al-Anon. A growing Al-Anon group now meets each week, and close relations with Alcoholics Anonymous and Al-Anon are maintained by all the centers of the state. Surprisingly court referrals have done well with us. This is probably because the referral is just that and not a compulsory commitment. The alcoholics from the courts have had the advantage of discussion with court personnel and have not simply been abruptly offered the alternative of being put in jail or being sent for enforced treatment. In most cases, if a patient had committed some serious offense—say, wrecked a car while speeding—he is appropriately sentenced for such offense and then encouraged to take part in a treatment program of the Bureau; simultaneously, he may take part in a remedial driver education course. This punishment seems to me to be just, although I do not believe that public drunkenness in itself should be regarded as a penal offense when that person is found by professionally competent authority to be an alcoholic.

The statewide public information program of the Bureau encourages problem drinkers to apply for treatment early at an outpatient clinic. These clinics thus constitute the first line of the intake process. The patient may then remain at the outpatient clinic, or if necessary, be admitted into a hospital for a time. After hospitalization ongoing therapy continues at an outpatient clinic.

Our endeavor is to make it possible for patients to attend a local community alcoholism program near their home. The patient usually continues to attend the clinic where he made his first contact, and the first contacting physician or counselor often becomes his outpatient therapist because of the initially established relationship. We do not yet have enough local programs in the state to bring all patients as close to a clinic as we would like; however, in general, in centers of population-density a patient does not have to go very far to keep his outpatient follow-up contacts.

The Admission Interview

What happens in the first interview or first few admission interviews is important. In fact, we consider the first telephone call, letter of inquiry, or appearance at a clinic vitally important. The voice at the clinic end represents help and that voice is trained to be sensitive to the caller's needs. The admitting or interviewing staff member, whether physician, social worker, psychologist, or other counselor must be able to listen understandingly. The admission interview must give the prospective patient or family member the opportunity really to say freely what he wishes; and the professional response must be one of helpfulness and realism, together with an offer of reasonable hope. No experienced or well-trained admitting officer ever makes the mistake, after listening for a few minutes, of offering pontifical "canned" advice on what the patient should do. Invariably, a prospective patient coming to an outpatient clinic is doing so with a degree of reluctance and anxiety, and under some social pressure. He may have had a sleepless night or several sleepless nights, wondering and worrying whether to take this step. He may have had to reinforce himself with a drink that morning or the day before, or he may have had quite a bit to drink the day before. He may be tremulous, shaky, and somewhat nauseated. He may feel desperately sorry for himself and remorseful and guilty. Whatever his state, a professional person has a crucial opportunity to listen and to accept the severity of the patient's complaints, and to recognize and to help the patient recognize that this is no minor matter.

As I have stated, patients are admitted on a voluntary basis; and no patient is formally committed, nor do the staff of the Bureau actually take part in committing any alcoholic patient, say, to a state hospital. When such commitment is considered advisable, it is recommended informally, then carried out through separate channels. We recognize, of course, that there are degrees of "voluntariness" and that an alcoholic patient is not likely to present himself for therapy unless he really is driven to do so by some inescapable crisis. He is in fact saying Yes and No at the same time. Pressures to confront the therapeutic opportunity are both internal and external: the patient is driven by his own anguish as well as threatened by his family or employer. The admission interview may, therefore, have to allow the patient to leave and return later when he fully realizes he needs help.

Not all external pressure is negative. There is evidence that reinforcement by employers may be effective not only in bringing a patient to therapy but also in determining favorable outcome. Pressure from the threat of job loss is sharply felt by prospective patients who have jobs that carry seniority and tenure rights. There are certain jobs, though, where this threat is minimal because the patient knows that he can go out and easily get another. We sometimes find in the admission interview that the patient is worried about his job but has not explained to his supervisor or employer why he has come to the hospital. The task of the interviewer in such an instance is to help the prospective patient face his employer with the facts if indicated in the particular case. A patient who comes into the hospital feeling that his boss is on his side and knows what is happening has made a great deal of progress already. In general, it is better that the patient rather than the counselor call the boss. Sometimes, it is wise for the interviewer to encourage the patient to call at once from the interviewing office, in which case they are both available to confer.

Most presenting patients give histories of progressively increasing difficulty related to drinking, usually for several years, and most applicants have previously been in private or state hospitals, or under the care of private physicians. Many, as I say, have been drinking and sometimes quite heavily within a day of admission; but most are, nonetheless, competent to make decisions about entry into therapy. Approximately 98 percent of those who apply are accepted for treatment by the Bureau; the rest are referred to other agencies. Psychiatric social workers, physicians, or other counselors take part in the initial task of helping the patient to accept therapy. The psychiatric social worker or the doctor may see both patient and spouse, as well as relatives. Family members may attend programs of an outpatient clinic for a considerable period of time. We see an increasing number of couples jointly with co-therapists present. Thus a physician and a psychiatric social worker may work together with a couple when this plan seems called for. They subsequently may want individual attention to be followed by a continuation of the couple interview.

It is very important that these intake procedures be carried out as expeditiously as possible so that patients do not have to wait any longer than absolutely necessary for beds or other care. In our service there is sometimes a waiting list, which causes delay and, therefore, anxiety to the prospective patient and his family. This is obviously something we must live with because there are simply not enough immediate services in any community, even by mobilizing all agencies, to care promptly for all needs. However, we do our best to see patients as early as possible after they make contact. We also try to establish early contact with the family's minister, if there is one, the family doctor, and other vitally concerned persons. As stated above, we always send reports of the patient's progress in the hospital and of our diagnostic findings (physical, psychological, and social) to the patient's physician. We hope by these reports to private physicians to aid them in the management and care of alcoholic patients in their own practice.

It is not the purpose of the Bureau to take over the whole care of the patient indefinitely or even at any time, but to share this with all relevant community resources. We are in constant touch with the patient's own professional advisers. We encourage professionals, both doctors and other caregivers, to visit our services when they are in the area. This enables us to come to know professionals throughout the state. We also take part in medical and other professional meetings and speak informally at churches, civic clubs, schools, and so forth.

The Bureau's philosophy of rehabilitation is based on the concept that there is a constellation of metabolic, psychological, socio-cultural, and spiritual factors operating in different proportions in every patient. We try to surround each patient and his family with a team of helpers, each with his own special field of competence. Thus our approach is interdisciplinary and comprehensive, including the patient as well as his family. We recognize that attention should not be given only to acute drinking problems but also to the concommitant job and family problems, as well as emotional and other problems of living and coping. We give careful attention to the readjustments of the patient and his family as the patient continues to remain abstinent. All or many of these concepts are discussed as early as possible with the patient and his family, sometimes, if appropriate, at the intake interview itself.

The processes of recruitment intake and of initiation into therapy play a significant part in the outcome of the therapy. It is not quite easy to say exactly what the key to a good referral interview or a good intake process is. Obviously, the personnel should be warm, accepting, and nonjudgmental, and at the same time realistic and objective. Obviously the prospective patient should be given an opportunity to speak freely about his presenting situation and should be encouraged to do so. Patients will sometimes show a tendency to deny and minimize their own drinking history; if the interviewing person is aware of this, he can handle the patient's minimization and denial without rejecting him. The patient should be encouraged to feel that his life is precious, valuable, and infinitely worth restoring through work in a cooperative relationship with a treatment team. Sometimes a prospective patient can feel that his denial and his "conning" are simply more evidence of the fact that he is no good. Sometimes the interviewing person can help the patient by letting him know that denial is a common mechanism, one that is evident and sometimes useful in our everyday lives, but when applied to such a big problem becomes a symptom. When the patient understands that he is not totally depraved in his denial, he begins to have hope. The patient then is more ready to understand that denial in this serious situation is not going to be helpful.

A patient should emerge from the intake interview or interviews with a sense that his illness is important, that he is indeed suffering from a condition that cannot be handled by denial or minimization. He also should leave the interviews knowing that the doctor or social worker or other counselors did not reject him by just patting him on the back, giving him some platitudes and superficial advice. In fact, the referral interview is no time to tell the patient exactly how his therapy is going to run. The counselor must let him know that there will be a good deal of testing and examining necessary to determine what the patient's problems are and what his assets are; that a plan will be worked out (a plan in which he will take part); and that a team will be set up of which he will be a leading member, or perhaps, *the* leading member. If possible, the patient should experience in the preliminary interviews the therapist's honest conviction that the patient is a worthwhile person, that his life is valuable, and that his value as a person is something that is not called into question. This approach to the patient's problem is what I would call truly professional. It is the view that a professional person should take about any illness or problem of a patient, no matter what it is. No moralistic quibbling or condemnation is ever justified. The alcoholic or problem drinker has a problem which partakes of the nature of illness; the patient should understand this. Armed with such understanding, he is now prepared to go on with treatment and hopefully make a success of it.

Hospitalization

In the Bureau the purpose of hospitalization is multifold. First, we make a detailed medical and psychological diagnostic evaluation within the supportive hospital environment. We use this evaluation to develop an individualized plan of long-term follow-up therapy in the outpatient clinic. In general, the inpatient phase of treatment is relatively brief, the patient remaining in the hospital no longer than is required to work out a satisfactory therapy program. It is always made clear to the patient that hospitalization is not the total treatment but is simply an introduction to it, an initation into what will continue afterward in the outpatient clinic and in other sources of help within the community. The objective of the hospital stay, then, is to initiate the rehabilitative process. We find that about a fourth of our patients are admitted from the outpatient clinic in an alcohol-free state, while the remainder are in a phase of postalcoholic withdrawal and a few in acute intoxication. It is not uncommon for us now to keep our patients in the hospital two or three weeks or sometimes even longer. (We formerly brought outpatients in for shorter periods than we do now that we have our new and larger inpatient Unit at the Medical College of Virginia.) The duration of a patient's stay in the hospital depends upon the particular needs of that patient. We wish to keep the patient in long enough to carry out the medical and psychological studies as well as make the psychiatric and social-work evaluation. This procedure usually takes, at the minimum, a week. We then like to have the patient remain at least a few days longer to take advantage of both daily group therapy and vocational rehabilitation counseling. We do not, however, wish the hospital stay to be more than an introduction into thse programs. Sometimes patients enter the hospital with the wrong impression, having had past experiences where the inpatient phase was considered the whole treatment. In such cases the patient may have been kept in the hospital for twenty-nine or thirty days and then turned loose with no further planned treatment at all. We believe this to be faulty procedure. However, if the patient has an acute alcohol intoxication when he comes in, he may have to remain longer. If he is in a postalcoholic withdrawal state, this too can mean a longer stay in the hospital. Job problems or an especially acute family crisis may also dictate a longer stay, though we do not attempt to solve these problems during hospitalization, we merely help him through the crisis situation. For this reason we require each patient to continue to receive therapeutic help in the outpatient clinic. We generally like the patient to attend the clinic on a regular basis for at least a year. We view the hospital stay, then, as an important initiation into a long-term therapy program and not as a domiciliary escape from the realities of his life situation.

Diagnosis

We shall discuss specifics of therapy as we proceed; here it is sufficient to note that the complexities of alcohol problems, as with any therapy, demand that treatment correspond to the diagnosed difficulties. Thus, as with any health problem, the diagnosis is essential in planning the therapeutic program with the patient and his family.

We obvioulsy use medication in the case of patients who are withdrawn and tremulous or in danger of suffering from delirium tremens, tremor, hallucinatory experience, or convulsions. Such pharmacological therapy is preventive and at the same time helps the patient to withdraw from alcohol use without excessive danger or unnecessary suffering. We never taper off patients or use alcohol therapeutically; we substitute for alcohol other much less dangerous substances. Moreover, most of these ataractic—that is to say, tranquilizing—drugs that we use do not act like alcohol. We also use a number of the new effective anti-depressant drugs. Our use of drugs, however, is conservative: they are used adjunctively as part of the total program of comprehensive treatment. The patients are also shown a series of therapeutic films and closed-circuit television programs, which provide information about their condition and the possibilities for change open to them through therapy. As soon as the patient enters the hospital he associates with both individuals and groups. The daily formal group therapy is reinforced by informal bull sessions among patients over coffee and by informal discussions with the nurses.

The Bureau works actively with Alcoholics Anonymous and other voluntary, local and state social agencies and health services. Members of A.A. visit with patients in the evenings on an informal basis. A thriving and vigorous regular A.A. group meets in the hospital ward every Thursday evening and is heavily attended. Patients are encouraged to attend A.A. meetings in the community on other evenings of the week.

Care

In the planned therapeutic milieu of our inpatient program, then, the patient is able to begin to explore his psychological and situational problems, form wholesome relationships, and experiment with a new way of life. Our large staff is competent and specialized. It includes internists, psychiatrists, general physicians, psychiatric social workers, vocational rehabilitation counselors, pastoral counselors, and many others who are in constant touch with the patients. We make free use of the consultative facilities of the university hospitals and invite consultations from internists, psychiatrists, and others in addition to our own staff.

Many alcoholic patients on admission are depressed, lonely, and beset with a sense of hopelessness and emptiness. Some patients present such symptoms without having had anything to drink for many days or weeks. A few patients may not have had anything to drink for many months or a year or more, although they are the exception. Sometimes patients will enter the hospital for a second or more time not directly because of drinking, but because they have experienced crises of other kinds. Although most of our patients are admitted with withdrawal symptoms, most are *compos mentis* and capable of making decisions. Patients usually come to the hospital with various acute situational difficulties connected with their work or families, or with psychosomatic or specific psychological and psychiatric disturbances.

In addition to full hospitalization, we accept a small number of day patients who may spend several days in the hospital participating in group activities by day and going to their own homes at night. We find that this program can be quite helpful, particularly for those who have been in the hospital before and who are attending outpatient clinics but who, for one reason or another, require the support of the hospital environment. Many patients refer to this experience as getting a "retread." Sometimes we find that patients are admitted as day patients simply because there is a waiting list and the patient needs immediate help to handle his tendency to drink or a recent drinking experience. We must admit, however, that this procedure is not really desirable. To admit as day patients those who are semi-intoxicated or withdrawing is hazardous. Such patients drink at night and come back the next day, and this simply becomes a defeating pattern. It is far better to have such a patient in the hospital for a twenty-four hour period each day. Daycare then is not a substitute for handling the withdrawing patient or the intoxicated patient; it is for those patients who are sober, yet need contact with group work within the hospital milieu. Sometimes, we do successfully "detoxify" certain patients in our out-patient clinic.

In addition to twenty-four-hour care and daycare, we also have nightcare plans whereby selected patients who have been in the hospital for several days may find it advantageous to work during the day in the community and come back in the evening for their supper and for evening group work. Through this procedure the patient is able to move gradually from the fulltime hospital environment to a fulltime community environment. Although this is used less frequently than we expected, the advantages are sometimes great: for example, nightcare can be very useful when a patient is going to a new job and needs regular encouragement and reassurance. Our evening clinics make it possible for such patients to be in contact with a physician for reinforcement of his motivation and for sharing his work experiences. Depression is a common symptom of many patients when they first enter the hospital. Only a small percentage of admitted patients present acute or chronic psychotic reactions. The most common is some form of hallucinosis. Fortunately, in the past few years, the proportion of patients who experience withdrawal convulsive reactions while in the hospital and who suffer from hallucinosis or delirium tremens is much reduced, due to new forms of medication. A number still suffer from tremors (the "shakes") during the first few days in hospital. Patients fall into most of the psychiatric diagnostic categories, including obsessive compulsive disorders, paranoid states, hysterical and neurotic reactions. A large proportion of our patients are passive, dependent individuals who find themselves overwhelmed and unable to function adequately. Many are hostile, suspicious, critical, and overwhelmed by their personal situations generally. Many appear to have a low tolerance to anxiety; they often reveal a wide gap between what they *say* and what they *do*. Many patients express little or no guilt, and seem to assume little or no sense or responsibility for personal choices. Many are not practical in making plans for themselves and often seek instant satisfaction and characteristically avoid painful situations. Many are also self-entrenched and withdrawn. Detached and apparently indifferent, they seem no longer to care and to have given up. We also find power-driven patients who seem to seek security through forcefulness, strength, and success. The latter often seem unable to acknowledge their need for help, but in actuality may be like the dependent and self-entrenched except for their uneasy solution in their own fancied omnipotence.

A large number of the patients fall into a category where they present neurotic and psychosomatic symptoms. These so-called somatization reactions are not uncommon, and the patients manifesting them seem to have settled into a reliance upon their own presumed physical illnesses. Often such retreat into somatic symptoms seems to serve one or another secondary gain. I was talking recently with a patient who displayed a whole series of symptoms that he regarded as extremely serious. He believed himself to have heart disease and other illnesses, and seemed content that these be considered legitimate cause for his retirement on sickness disability. Actually, the patient is in quite good physical condition, but he cannot surrender his somatic reactions because of what they apparently do for him.

We are constantly involved in clinical studies. One of these is an ongoing project to attempt to correlate these somatic symptoms and other diagnostic categorizations with eventual treatment outcome. One gains the impression that alcoholics are often meticulous about medical and dental checkups, grossly neglecting the harm they do by their drink-ing.

The new inpatient-outpatient facility at the Medical College of Virginia, Virginia Commonwealth University, which we shall describe in further detail below, has made it possible for us to mount a comprehensive program of rehabilitation. We are capable of working with forty inpatients at a time and are hoping, in addition, for a further ten-bed detoxification unit. This unit will be manned by staff devoted to the specialized problem of treating coma, and so forth in alcoholic patients. At present we operate about sixteen beds for entering patients who need the shelter of their rooms by day as well as by night. These patients may be intoxicated or they may be in a withdrawal, jittery, tremulous state, but all of them are capable of being treated on a voluntary basis. These patients are seen by the internists of our division with consultation from other departments when necessary. Generally speaking, we make free use of consultative services of the whole medical center; but by and large, we are sufficiently able to deal with most of the medical, social, and psychiatric needs of our patients ourselves. Sometimes we find it appropriate to transfer a patient to another department, particularly medicine and psychiatry, often with the plan of having him returned to us after his particular problem has been dealt with by the more specialized resources of the other department.

The present new service also includes a well-appointed, well-staffed outpatient clinic. This clinic operates five days a week, eight hours a day, and also includes four evening sessions two nights a week. Former patients and other volunteers who are appropriately trained are counselors during the day or the evening.

10
A Working Model (Cont'd)

The Therapeutic Community

The hospital community in which treatment starts is housed in a modern, 40-bed living unit comprised of 16 conventional beds for acutely ill patients who need to be in bed during the day. The other 24 patients occupy attractive, two-bed rooms with sofa beds, made to resemble living rooms or college dormitories. These patients are active participants of the therapeutic community, taking part in all group activity. There is an increasing tendency for patients to require fewer and fewer days confined to bed. Patients not so incapacitated make their own beds and serve their own food. Meals are a particularly happy and free time, with no restrictions except for the dietary prescriptions outlined for each patient. They may eat in a small dining room, or in groups of two or three in their own rooms, or in a group of about sixteen in the recreation lounge (which also serves as a closed-circuit television room and a group-therapy room). There is also a smaller lounge, beautifully furnished in contemporary style which holds as many as eight patients for a meal. Thus, instead of a single large cafeteria, we offer a variety of arrangements, which allows patients to select the amount of socialization they desire. Although staff members do not eat their meals regularly on the ward, they do sometimes share coffee with the patients informally. Since we have also made it a practice to have food available to patients at all times, we keep refrigerators stocked with milk, butter, eggs, ham, and cheese so that patients may have snacks whenever they wish. Such access to food has been particularly useful for patients who are malnourished or who have specific vitamin deficiencies.

Thus, there is a maximum of forty patients under full-time hospital care. This number includes only the nightcare patients, however, and not the extra patients we can accommodate during the day. Those 24 patients in the community self-care area participate in group work while the sixteen patients confined to their rooms during the day are visited by staff members, and participate with the nurses in simple group work. For the most part, patients move from the hospital-type rooms to the therapeutic community self-care units within three or four days after admission.

All inpatients participate in a program of patient government where opportunity is given to air grievances, make suggestions, and share ideas. Nurses are increasingly taking leadership with patients in handling such problems as drinking on the ward and other issues that arise in living together under such close conditions, so that there is a mutual learning experience between nurse and patient from which both benefit in the end.

Group Work: General Approach (Hoff [12])

Work with patients in groups, particularly in the inpatient phase, is conducted daily and sometimes more than once a

day. A main objective of this group work is to cement together the members of the therapeutic community, as well
as to motivate action, to handle anxieties and psychological
problems, and to encourage abstinence. While group techniques do have the effect of maximizing staff utilization,
this is not a major objective. In other words, we do not use
group techniques simply to make up for any inadequacy of
qualified staff.

Within the intimately knit therapeutic community of the
inpatient service—a community continually changing through
new admission and discharge of patients—there is an ongoing interaction among the patients themselves and between
patients and staff. Thus the inpatient group sessions serve
primarily to provide some cohesiveness to the community
and accurate, readily understandable information about
the programs and procedures of the Unit, the day-to-day
activities, and the functions of staff members. Approximately once a week, we show a recent one-half hour color
film called *Alcohol, The Number One Drug Addiction,* produced and filmed in our Unit in 1973. In this film staff members and former patients (who have signed releases for their
appearance) depict and comment on our thereapeutic program and its general activities. Partly because it is so recent,
this film generates lively discussion.

In addition, we regularly schedule five or six new films and
tapes throughout each week on subjects such as the nature,
course, and prevention of alcoholism, the use of Antabuse, and
so on. One film in particular *Profile of a Problem Drinker* (Alcoholism and Addiction Foundation, Ontario, Canada), a nar-
rative story about a young man and his wife who seek help,
is presented about once a week, and even though a little out of
date, serves to evoke discussions which the group leader can
then focus on the group itself. It has been found that the presentation of this kind of neurophysiological and psychological

information has great value in encouraging patients in the group to express their own psychological and family problems.

We have observed that the morale generated and fostered by inpatient group sessions sets up a wholesome contagion that quickly draws new patients into the ward community. The milieu of the group sessions appears to be less threatening than individual sessions, especially for new patients. Very often group interaction and intragroup support encourage the patients to express feelings of depression, fear, anger, guilt, confusion, and inadequacy, as well as to talk about their hopes and plans. In the inpatient groups (as well as in the outpatient groups to be described later), patients are frequently motivated by the group meetings to seek special individual sessions with staff and to ask for conferences with members of their family, their employers, and other relevant persons. Dynamic processes in group work thus radiate to individual sessions which in turn evoke feedback in the group sessions.

Similar dynamics operate in the outpatient clinic group situation. In both group settings, unresolved problems that are brought openly to the fore in the group session, that demand immediate attention, are handled as soon as possible, either while the session is in progress or directly after the session is completed.

We have found that a meaningful and practical objective of group work is to enhance motivation for the sobriety which will lead to a more satisfying way of life. The thrust seems always to be "How can I make tomorrow a better day than the last?" The subject matter of group discussion is freely chosen, but tends to have a certain pattern as the week goes by. Many patients who are new to the inpatient group will talk about "Why I drink." Then, a few days later the patients begin to adopt the view that the first order of priority is to stop drinking regardless of the reasons. This development comes about as the patient continues in sobriety, for as his physical and mental condition improves, he can then develop insight and handle situations more effectively. Thus, it is usual in both inpatient and outpatient group work to deal with situations as they come up on a day-to-day basis. We believe that within both the inpatient and outpatient groups, growing understanding of their problems strengthens motivation.

Finally, the group setting seems to be favorable in helping patients to make plans, to take inventory of their lives, and to learn some of the principles of orderly problem solving. The limitations of group work are shared with the patients. Their own expectations for the group are assessed and freely discussed. Inpatients are encouraged to look upon group therapy as an integral part of the total therapeutic program which is balanced by private sessions that afford opportunities for individual help not available in the group. The outpatient groups as well are encouraged to view group work as only one element in an integrated plan that includes individual work with the clinic physician and/or social worker, as well as pastoral or other counseling, and participation in Alcoholics Anonymous. Thus we do not present group work in any setting as a sole or isolated therapeutic modality.

Inpatient Group Work

Duration of hospitalization for our patients is determined by a number of factors all related to the patients' needs and capabilities. Since hospitalization is relatively brief—from one to three weeks—there is a rapid turnover in the inpatient group. The group is often entirely new every two weeks, and there is hardly a session in which one or more new patients are not added. There are group work sessions in some form every day, and under the present arrangement, I myself join with alcoholism therapists as cotherapist in psychodrama two days a week—Thursday and Friday. On Tuesday the senior social worker leads the group work either by herself or with her field-work students in social work or with alcoholism counselors. Because of the daily shifting of the group, each session comes to have a meaning and value of its own.

We used to think that it would be difficult to evoke strong feelings of group interaction in the inpatient session partly because of patients' recent drinking damaging the nervous system, but this has not proved to be the case. In fact, the inpatients think of group therapy as a real factor in bringing them together as more open people. Many of them say that if it were not for the formal daily group sessions their informal evening bull sessions over dinner and coffee, for example, would be less active. Patients use such expressions as "family" to describe the relationship they feel. The fact that they will interrupt this relationship within a few weeks, for some reason does not seem to carry a negative effect. Many tell us that they later rediscover and apply in their homes and work situations what they acquire in the group from day to day. Others find that A.A. is more meaningful to them after having patient group experience; some will come back to visit favorite groups because they want to revitalize their experience of the group relationships.

The outpatient groups, however, which are composed of the same members month after month have certain advantages over the inpatient group with its more rapid turnover. In the inpatient group each session imposes an imprint of permanent value, yet relatively unrelated to the duration of the group experience. It cannot be denied that the inpatient meetings participated in by new patients who have lately suffered from various effects of drinking do not generate the insight and serenity of subsequent outpatient sessions.

An account of a typical week will serve to illustrate our use of group work in the hospital service. First, there is a staff conference ("briefing" session) four days a week, Tuesday through Friday at 9:30 in the morning. All patients admitted the previous day are seen and have an opportunity to talk freely about themselves and learn of the program as it may apply to them. They are informed of the length and nature of hospitalization, outpatient follow-up, use of medications, and other issues that may not have been settled at the prior admission interview, particularly if the patient had been intoxicated.

On Monday morning at 10:30 in our Unit there is an Al-Anon meeting for families of alcoholics. This program is new and we encourage inpatients and their spouses to come and join these groups. Also, a number of Al-Anon members in the community attend. Our hope is that as time goes on this Al-Anon group will become stabilized and a regular part of our program. Every Monday morning at 9:30 there is a group session held by the inpatients and lead by the chief nurse or her assistant. This meeting is an important beginning of each week because it deals with patient government. The principles and practices of patient government are discussed, new officers are elected, and special problems are brought up, such as "gripes" about the service and drinking on the ward. Hopefully some of these can be solved by patients' cooperation with each other.

On Monday afternoon the physician in charge of the inpatient service leads a general discussion on the effects of alcohol and the use of Antabuse and other medication. Usually this develops into a lively meeting and helps new patients, particularly, to know something more about what their program in the inpatient service and *afterwards* is going to be liked. Every Monday, Wednesday, and Friday, the chief resident chaplain of the Department of Patient Counseling of the Medical College who is attached full-time to our Unit, holds inpatient group sessions. Also, as one of his duties he operates a training program for local clergymen who work with inpatients in our Unit under his supervision. In this program four positions are available for a sixteen-week course offered twice a year.

In addition, a staff member leads lively transactional analysis groups on Tuesday and Wednesday afternoons for inpatients and on Monday and Thursday evenings for outpatients. Also there are two Alcoholics Anonymous meetings each week in the service. The one on Monday evening at 8:00 is a somewhat informal discussion group. A more formal group, a regular group of the Richmond area, of which we are very proud, meets in the hospital at 8:30 every Thursday evening These A.A. meetings are open to both inpatients and outpatients as well as to members of the public at large.

We orient the therapeutic community in such a way as to encourage new patients to enter into group work as quickly as possible after admission. Patients in the therapeutic community tend to spend a very small proportion of their daytime hours in their own rooms or in bed but are actively engaged in appointments for tests, both medical and psychodiagnostic, in formal therapeutic sessions, in recreation or informal sessions over coffee. The special activities program of the Department of Occupational Therapy (Special Services) is in the same building, and patients use these facilities as prescribed for them. This Department also provides entertainment films within the precincts of our service which patients are at liberty to attend.

For the past year or more, we have gathered together a group of alcoholism counselors and other staff on Thursdays and Fridays to lead an inpatient program of psychodrama. This psychodramatic effort has been quite successful and it serves particularly to free up patients and encourage them to confront each other and expose and release their emotions in a healthy, positive fashion. The format is generally a traditional one. It permits patients not only to express their feelings but also to act out problems they face but do not know how to handle otherwise. Since the psychodramatic sessions are held at the end of the week, they come, for some, very close to their discharge from the inpatient service and are thus useful when confronting immediate difficulties with their families, their employers, and their friends. If a particular dramatic session is not resolved on the Thursday session there is time to take it up again on Friday. The "stars" are interchangeable, several patients taking the part, say, of a husband or of a wife or of a boss so that everyone who wants to has a chance to see how he would play it out. Between the action sessions there are breaks in which the group vigorously discusses whether the session was realistic or not and makes active suggestions for changes. Psychodrama appeals to people and takes advantage of natural tendencies to be a "ham." In addition these sessions are innovative and appealing to the large number of students and trainees who attend the Unit. In summary of our discussion of inpatient group work, it should be said that many patients who have the leisure are invited to return to various inpatient group therapy sessions for further experience.

Outpatient Group Work

A group of men and women patients was organized in September, 1964, and has been meeting each Monday evening since then with additions and deletions. All the members of this group are presently working or have worked in the past individually with other staff members of the outpatient clinic. I speak of this group since it is the pioneer of the outpatient groups in our program. The only condition for entry into the group is a personal wish to join and an agreement to stay with it for at least six months. The patients also agree to report in by telephone in advance, if there is some special reason for absence from a meeting. At any time after six months, a patient may voluntarily withdraw from the group. We usually maintain a maximum of fifteen patients, and presently four patients have been in the group since its inception. There is, therefore, a core of old members and, on the whole, the group organization is quite stable. This is a semi-closed group which, at the time of its organization, evolved for itself the concept that therapy would be by the group as a whole for the members of the group; and this objective has been quite consistently followed. Usually each member of the group will report on incidents that have happened during the past week and how he or she has been getting along in his day-to-day living. Ordinarily at a meeting, one patient or possibly two will bring up special matters upon which they desire the counsel of the group. In this kind of transaction it turns out that one or two members will take leadership in the counseling, but it is rare for anyone to maintain complete silence. The sessions are quite informal, and although existential issues are ordinarily uppermost in the discussion, it frequently happens that basic questions on the cause, course, and treatment of alcoholism and principles of problem solving and psychodynamics will be brought up. This outpatient group never begins with any particular agenda. Over the years the group has become quite close-knit, and members will sometimes see each other outside the clinic.

When a new patient is brought into the group temporarily for special support, certain members will rally around him, help him get a job and a place to stay, and befriend him. I am thinking of a particular member of our outpatient group, a man who has been in the group only a little over a month. He is an enthusiast and has gotten a number of jobs for people. One or two of the older members reacted negatively to his enthusiasm, which has mellowed him and modified his tendency toward extremes. On the whole, then, I think he will make a good member of the group because of his willingness to help; and if he will take advantage of the greater experience of the older members of the group, as I believe he will, he can become a useful person. When he is not working, he often comes to the inpatient service and is of help there in talking with new patients and making himself useful generally. We consider the outpatient Monday evening group as a training program for persons who can act as paraprofessional aides. The outpatient group sometimes discusses what goes on in the inpatient group and stands ready to come into the inpatient group with their greater experience. This is precisely what our new patient in the outpatient group is doing right now. From time to time, inpatients in the ward are invited to share meetings with the outpatient group.

The outpatient group has experimented with psychodramatic techniques but has not adopted them consistently, although on occasion members of the outpatient group have come to the inpatient group to participate in psychodrama.

We have observed that the main cues for psychodramatic themes arise from the discussions within the inpatient sessions, but sometimes the cues come from films that have been shown either that day or the day before. Often the film *Profile of a Problem Drinker* has suggested topics for psychodrama. When this happens, it can become a dominant concern for several days, the group members offering variations of the situation in the film. When the inpatient group so wishes, tape recordings of the psychodramatic sessions are made, some of them fairly elaborate. Taping or recording an individual or group session is always done with the agreement of the patients. We have yet to experiment with the filming or video taping of patients in acute intoxication. Investigation of this kind of recording is a research project which we hope eventually to undertake.

Other Group Approaches

The Unit continues to study and experiment in the field of group relationships. For instance, as mentioned before we are experimenting with the technique of "couple therapy," in which a therapist and co-therapist join, for example, with a husband and wife in a four-way therapeutic session. Such group work has value as well as limitations and we try to capture the values.

I have been struck by the fact that some patients on entering inpatient service tend to want to stay in their rooms and isolate themselves. The group work seems to them at first to be unhelpful and they may criticize it. More than likely, however, within two or three days this attitude changes. Last Friday, for example, a group session dealt with "the rewards of abstinence." Patients realistically brought up how difficult abstinence is and how the rewards of drinking seem much more obvious. Nevertheless, one patient, who had previously insisted on staying in his room, joined the group and reported later that he really felt it was the beginning of a new, more constructive way of life.

The 1969 Center

In 1969, as stated, the General Assembly of Virginia appropriated monies to establish this Unit at the Medical College of Virginia as a Center not only to treat and rehabilitate but also to work with the Medical College of Virginia (Virginia Commonwealth University) to study and investigate on a comprehensive basis causes, treatment and prevention of alcoholism and to educate and train doctors, nurses, social workers, alcoholism counselors and research workers. The Legislation signaled a step forward in the growing attention paid to serious social and health problems of alcoholism and problem drinking. Clinical study of patients has been backed up by neurophysiological studies since the creation of the Division of Neurological and Psychiatric Research at the Medical College of Virginia which has devoted itself since 1946 largely to problems relating to addiction. As head of this research Division as well as the clinical Unit, I have attempted to integrate the research laboratories intimately with the clinical services. Over the years these research programs have been well staffed and supported by national grants as well as by State appropriations. Our clinical Unit includes facilities for research into causes and diagnosis as well as new methods of treatment of drinking problems. There are facilities for detoxification and the study of these patients. We are equipped with an inpatient therapeutic community-living Unit to experiment with the many types of group therapy I have discussed. In addition, other treatment methods are being explored by members of the staff. Daycare facilities permit evaluation of treatment without hospitalization and there are transitional treatment stages as well as outpatient care. Our Unit includes attractive conference areas for teaching and instruction and we are gradually acquiring staff adequate to perform our clinical and educational functions. We regularly receive staff from other Centers of the Bureau around the State for indoctrination and training at the request of local centers. These relationships are felicitous because not only is it possible to exchange and share ideas, but also they facilitate referral of patients. One of the research projects that we have undertaken has been to investigate the best means for promoting flow of patients.

I have previously mentioned some of the issues that have come up in relation to operating multiracial services. We are proud of this feature of our program. For example, on an experimental basis we operate two special integrated outpatient clinics in the Medical College of Virginia Unit. These are heavily attended and both have a high success rate. There is evidence that sometimes the success rate of the black patients is higher than the white, and sometimes it is the other way around. Using sustained abstinence as a criterion of success, we have found a success rate of about ninety percent. I believe, as I have said before, that the satisfactory outcome of treatment in these two clinics held on Tuesday and Friday afternoons is due to the fact that we make available to all of the patients, black or white, treatment for their hypertension as well as their seizures. Both seizures and hypertension are "spin offs" of alcoholism and both unfortunately have a higher incidence among black people whether alcoholic or not. It has been gratifying to monitor the real sense of returning and persisting health amongst all patients who suffer from these two illnesses complicating their alcoholism.

A top priority in our program is special education and training. We train nurses and dietitians; we offer training for undergraduate physicians and also graduate doctors, particularly young psychiatrists. I have already referred to our training of clergy and I should mention also our satisfaction with our alcoholism counselor trainees, most of whom have A.A. background. In our training programs, we act under the direction of Mr. Ed Mulligan in charge of training for the Bureau of Alcohol Studies and Rehabilitation in the entire State. For the past four years we have been receiving social work students of Virginia Commonwealth University for field work in their first or second years, which has been a rewarding program.

Since the entire number of patients in our Center is at any one time limited, we recognize that the program should be designed not simply to treat, but also to demonstrate therapeutic and other techniques for helping patients. Obviously many of the patients that we must be concerned about in the State are those that we will not ever be able to treat ourselves. However, our Unit is in a position to provide assistance to local hospitals and local professional people and to furnish research studies that may be helpful. Teams from our Unit are prepared to assist and advise on the establishment of facilities in other parts of the State. Some of these are not necessarily related to the Bureau of Alcohol Studies and Rehabilitation directly, but involve, for example, cooperative relations with Federal treatment programs. We stand ready at all times to consult with staffs of community hospitals as to how our respective facilities can be made more effective and how we can participate in programs with State and local health facilities.

Apart from our research interests, touched on in this chapter and elsewhere, in one of my preoccupations has been with the deteriorated, isolated, homeless men whom we have often mistitled, "skid row alcoholics." I have watched with great anticipation some of the good work that the governments of various states and nations are carrying out for these unfortunate people. I think that one of the places to do research studies on alcoholism is among those who exhibit the illness in its most devastating form, and I hope that in the case of the homeless man, such studies will pay off. I can remember some twenty years ago it was generally stated that the success rate for homeless alcoholics, taken as a whole, was given at about four or five percent. Let us fervently hope that our growing skills will enable us to elevate that rate considerably.

In 1949, I became interested in the use of Disulfiram (Antabuse). This is a remarkable drug which holds out hope for deterring people from drinking. We have used the drug ourselves since then and have been generally satisfied with its therapeutic efficacy. From 1950 to 1955 we carried out a study of a total of 1187 alcoholics, 1020 patients who took Antabuse, and 484 controls who did not. In this study we offered Antabuse as an adjunct in treatment and matched these with alcoholic patients who did not take the drug but whose treatment was otherwise similar. All of the patients were administered the drug voluntarily and were not given Antabuse unless they requested it. All of the patients had been drinking progressively and more and more seriously in an uncontrolled fashion, usually for several years. Most of them had previously been under treatment in private sanatoria, state hospitals or with private physicians. Most of them had been drinking within the day prior to admission.

All of the patients received a test for Antabuse-alcohol reaction. This was accomplished by giving alcohol to the patient who had been taking Antabuse for a few days previously. There is a fall in systolic and diastolic blood pressure and a corresponding rise in pulse rate together with increase in the rate of breathing as well as nausea and other symptoms. These unpleasant responses occurred within about ten minutes after taking alcohol on top of Antabuse and are due to the action of the Antabuse in blocking one stage of the breakdown processes of alcohol in the liver. In a heavy reaction there is shortness of breath, coughing, pounding of the heart, tingling and numbness of the hands and in some cases dizziness, visual blurring and a pound-frontal headache. Presently in our Unit we do not give an Antabuse-alcohol reaction, but simply tell the patients what it is like and the results are equally effective. There have been no dire reactions or fatalities due to use of the drug.

Comparing the 1020 Antabuse cases with the 484 controls, we see that 76.5 percent of the Antabuse patients have definitely benefited by treatment, while 55.0 percent of the controls are so classified. The Antabuse cases also have a better record of follow-up. Thus, Antabuse patients do significantly better than controls according to statistical tests. In all of our studies of male-female differences, male patients do significantly better than females. Of the male Antabuse patients 77.4 percent did better while 67.3 percent of the females who took Antabuse showed improvement. In our earlier studies of alcoholic patients there were consistently poorer results for patients under 30 in either the Antabuse or control groups. However, more complete, longer term studies now indicate that patients under 30 have nearly but not quite as good a record as the total groups (Hoff [17, 18, 19]).

Alcoholics younger than 30 are occupying a higher and higher percentage of the population and the problem of the young alcoholic is indeed one which must be taken seriously. We are working with large numbers of younger alcoholics in our Unit. We need to know more about why young people take to alcohol and how they become addicted, possibly transferring from some other drug.

Perhaps the most important of all studies, not only in the interest of better treatment of alcoholics but also in the eradication of alcoholism, are detailed and sophisticated studies of genetic factors in alcoholism and in the relationships between alcoholism and the ways in which children grow up in families or without families. We must be deeply concerned about the effects of emotional, financial and educational deprivation on young people and upon their subsequent capacity to tolerate life without recourse to the chemical comfort of alcohol (16).

Not only do problem drinkers (especially women) owe their unhappiness in many cases to early affectional and other emotional deprivation, but also a large number have grown up without the wholesome, healthy support of the church whose responsibility for prevention of alcoholism is a very heavy one. We should be grateful for the good and continuing work done in the direction of prevention by the North Conway Institute, whose executive director is The Reverend David A. Works. (13, 14) and the Middle Atlantic Institute of Alcohol and Other Drug Studies in Richmond under the guidance for many years of The Reverend Dr. Wayne W. Womer.

Epilogue

This afternoon I received a telephone call from a quiet, well-spoken young woman asking earnestly for help for her abnormal drinking. She had previously been a patient in two distinguished psychiatric centers on the East Coast. She was fearful of taking her own life. The young woman's desperate appeal, to which I immediately responded, exemplifies the seriousness of alcoholism not only as a cause of continuing, chronic suffering, misery, and depression but also as a life-threatening emergency. Here is an affliction that *gives rise to* terrible unhappiness, and, in addition, *thrives in* a climate of deprivation and frustration. Thus, the *Cooperative Commission on the Study of Alcoholism* (4) has recommended that alcholism may possibly be reduced by lowering the rates of psychological disorders and by improving mental heatlh. This is why it is vital to improve the quality of family life, provide preventive crisis intervention for individuals and families, and increase understanding of human emotions and of interpersonal relations.

Outstanding in our country today is an urgent need for a renewed sense of community, a loving, neighborly respect and concern in which people can realize their own potentials with ample room to express diversity. A potent approach to prevention of alcoholism lies in no less than the creation of a better and more humane society. In such a society, one can expect fewer problem drinkers. I believe alcoholism can be lessened by elimination of poverty, provision of equal opportunity for all, insurance of social justice, establishment of adequate preventive and curative medical services, and reduction of feelings of alienation. These goals are shared by all and ought to be pursued for their own sake, as well as for their impact upon many disorders, including alcoholism.

It is profoundly encouraging that new and comprehensive community alcoholism plans are being developed throughout the country, drawing together wide varieties of agencies, both private and public, and at several levels of government. These plans include treatment and prevention through more efficient delivery of services, through education, and through research. Most especially gratifying is a growing public willingness to support such plans.

References

1. McCarthy, Raymond G. *Exploring Alcohol Questions.* (One of six pamphlets in a series by the same title.) Yale Center of Alcohol Studies: New Haven, Connecticut.
2. Ford, J. C. *Man Takes a Drink: Facts and Principles About Alcohol.* Kennedy: New York, 1956.
3. Jellinek, E. M. *The Disease Concept of Alcoholism.* College and University Press: New Haven, Connecticut. (Fifth printing), 1972.
4. Plaut, Thomas F. A. *Alcohol Problems: A Report to the Nation by the Cooperative Commission on the Study of Alcoholism.* Oxford University Press: New York, 1967.
5. Jellinek, E. M. "Symposium on Therapy of Alcohol Addiction: Introduction," *Quart. J. Stud. Alc.* 5 (1944), pp. 185-188.
6. Hoff, E. C. "The Etiology of Alcoholism," *Quart. J. Stud. Alc.,* Supplement No. 1 (1961), pp. 57-65.
7. Witkin, H. A., Karp, S. A. and Goodenough, D. R. "Dependence in alcoholics," *Quart. J. Stud., Alc.* 20 (1959), pp. 493-504.
8. Hoff, E. C. "Higher Cerebral Regulation of Autonomic Function: A Historical Perspective." In: Hockman, Charles, *Limbic Influences on Autonomic Function.* Charles C. Thomas: Springfield, Ill., 1971.
9. Jellinek, E. M. *Phases in the Drinking History of Alcoholics.* No. 5, Memoirs of the Section of Studies on Alcohol. Yale University Press: New Haven, Connecticut, 1946.
10. Thiebout, Harry M. "Alcoholics Anonymous—An Experiment of Nature," *Quart. J. Stud. Alc.* 22 (1961), pp. 52-68.
11. Virginia, Commonwealth of, *An Act of the General Assembly of Virginia providing for study of problems of alcoholism, treatment of persons addicted to excessive use of alcohol,*

establishment of a Division of Alcohol Studies and Rehabilitation, Richmond, Va. Virginia State Department of Health, 1948.

12. Hoff, E. C. "Group Therapy With Alcoholics," *Psychiatric Research Report 24* (March, 1968), American Psychiatric Association, Chapter V, pp. 61-70.

13. North Conway Institute, *Alcohol and the American Churches,* Boston, Mass., 1967.

14. North Conway Institute, *Alcohol and Church Programs: 21 Case Studies of Community, State and National Programs.* Boston, Mass., 1968.

15. Virginia State Department of Health, Bureau of Alcohol Studies and Rehabilitation, *The Comprehensive Community Alcoholism Plan for the State of Virginia.* Richmond, Virginia, 1974.

16. Hoff, E. C. *Decisions About Alcohol.* Seabury Press: New York, 1965.

17. Hoff, E. C. "The Rehabilitation of Chronic Alcoholics," *Trans. Acad. Med. N. J.,* (I. *Alcoholism, Modern Concepts of Cause and Therapy* 1-107) 79-84, 1972.

18. Hoff, E. C. "The Psychological and Pharmacological Basis for the Treatment of Alcohol Dependency," pp. 383-421. In: Israel, Yedy, *Biological Basis of Alcoholism.* John Wiley and Sons, Inc.: New York, 1971.

19. Hoff, E. C. "The Use of Pharmacological Adjuncts in the Comprehensive Therapy of Alcoholics," pp. 240-262, In: Whitney, Elizabeth D., *World Dialogue on Alcohol and Drug Dependence.* Beacon Press: Boston, 1970.

Suggestions for Further Reading

BOOKS

American Medical Association. *Manual on Alcoholism.* AMA, New York, 1968, 95 pp.

Bacon, Margaret and Mary Brush Jones. *Teen-Age Drinking.* Thomas Y. Crowell Company, New York, 1968, 228 pp.

Cork, R. Margaret. *The Forgotten Children.* Addiction Research Foundation, 1969, 112 pp.

Hoff, E. C. "Higher Cerebral Regulation of Autonomic Function: A Historical Perspective" in Charles Hockman, *Limbic Influences on Autonomic Function.* Charles C. Thomas, Springfield, Ill., 1971.

Hornik, Edith L. *You and Your Alcoholic Parent.* Association Press, New York, 1974, 127 pp.

Mann, Marty. *New Primer on Alcoholism.* New York, Holt, Rinehart and Winston, 1958, 235 pp.

Seixas, Frank A., Remi Cadoret, and Suzie Eggleston. *The Person with Alcoholism.* Proceedings of the Fourth Medical-Scientific Conference by NCA, April, 1973. Annals of the New York Academy of Sciences, vol. 233, New York, 1974.

Straus, Robert. *Alcohol and Society.* Reprinted from *Psychiatric Annals,* Special Edition, 1973, 60 pp.

U.S. Department of Health, Education & Welfare. *Alcohol and Health.* DHEW Publication No. (HSM) 72-9099, Washington, D.C., 1971, 121 pp.

PAMPHLETS

American Medical Association. *The Illness Called Alcoholism.* AMA, New York, 1973, 13 pp.

Criteria Committee, National Council on Alcoholism. *Criteria for the Diagnosis of Alcoholism.* Reprinted from *American Journal of Psychiatry,* 129:2, August, 1972, 9 pp.

Milt, Harry. *Alcoholics and Alcoholism.* National Council on Alcoholism, New York, Public Affairs Pamphlet No. 426, 1967, 25 pp.

National Council on Alcoholism. *What Are the Signs of Alcoholism?* NCA, New York, 1972, 3 pp.

NIMH/NIAAA. *Alcohol and Alcoholism: Problems, Programs and Progress.* NIMH/NIAAA, Rev. 1972, 42 pp.

Seixas, Frank A. *A Local Habitation and A Name.* Reprinted from *Rhode Island Medical Journal,* 55: 71-76, March, 1972, 7 pp.